Satish Kumar is Chairman of the Schumacher Society and Editor of the journal *Resurgence*, with which Dr Schumacher was closely associated and which is concerned with fostering a long-term vision of the social change embodied in Schumacher's work. His autobiography, *No Destination*, was published in 1978.

Satish Kumar lives in  e smallholding.

E. F. Schumacher titles from ABACUS:

SMALL IS BEAUTIFUL
GOOD WORK
A GUIDE FOR THE PERPLEXED

THE SCHUMACHER LECTURES

Edited with an Introduction by
Satish Kumar

Abacus edition published in 1982
by Sphere Books Ltd
30/32 Gray's Inn Road, London WC1X 8JL

First published in Great Britain by
Blond & Briggs Ltd 1980
Copyright © 1980 The Schumacher Society

Printed and bound in Great Britain by
Cox & Wyman Ltd, Reading

Contents

Introduction

The challenge Dr Schumacher has left for us to meet is not to stop at the generalities of the goodness in 'small', but to take the concept in concrete terms and see how, in practice, small is workable and possible in health, in education, in agriculture, in commerce and industry.

One danger we face in this world of specialization is that we tend to take only one aspect or one dimension of reality and think of it as total reality. Like those blind men who met a certain animal and each of whom touched a different part of its body – legs, ears, trunk, tail and so on. When they gathered together to describe the animal, they all had totally different ideas of what the animal looked like. The one who had touched the leg thought it was a pillar. The one who had touched the tail thought of it as a thin hanging rope. The one who had touched the trunk thought of it as a fat crusty worm. In this way all of them kept arguing and quarrelling with each other without knowing the whole animal – the total elephant.

The friends of the late Dr Schumacher seem to be in the same boat. Some of us see him as a champion of intermediate and appropriate technology; others see him as an exponent of organic farming; there are others who see him as a prophet of new economics; and still others consider him the apostle of ecology, environment and alternative sources of energy. But none of us seem able to see the total man and beyond – beyond his personality. It is not good enough just to offer him a few words of praise. We must open ourselves to see the multidimensional reality.

Therefore it is an apt tribute to Fritz Schumacher that we have six memorial lectures, and two additional papers, which individually and collectively represent that totality – the holistic vision. Here we have the vision of R. D. Laing, who on the surface may appear to be concerned with the internal reality, but that is only on the surface. His ideas and experiences of reality are in total harmony with the external realities of our planet. In the same way, the concerns of Amory Lovins for soft energy and Ivan Illich's concerns for deschooling, medical nemesis and conviviality appear to be in the sphere of the external world. But that is only an appearance. In truth they touch the core of personal, social and cosmic existence. Similarly, John Michell's plea to take a long view of history and not get hooked on Darwin, Fritjof Capra's call to liberate ourselves from the Newtonian past, and Edward de Bono's warning to guard against strait-jacket thinking all form part of that same holistic vision.

What is the sign of a great man? A person whose head is high above in the clouds, whose vision can reach the ultimate reality, but at the same time whose feet are grounded in the soil of intimate experience, who is practical, simple and able to communicate with people of every kind. E. F. Schumacher was one such great man.

Born in Bonn, he had been a Rhodes Scholar in Oxford in the 1930s and finally settled in England permanently. He started his life not as an academic but as a farm labourer, learning from the soil and nature. It was then that he started to ponder on the relationship between technology and the modern practice of farming as if money were all that mattered. He later became an economic adviser to the British Control Commission in Germany, followed by twenty years with the National Coal Board.

His stay in Burma and India was the breakthrough point. While helping on the programme of rural development he found that most of the planners and advisers were advocating economic growth through labour-saving and capital-intensive technology, although labour was available in abundance and capital was scarce. What a crazy situation! Schumacher's advice to the governments and the planners in India and Burma was to find an indigenous way of development and to pursue the path of capital-saving, labour-intensive intermediate technology.

In the 1950s and 1960s when economic growth was the demigod of the planners and when technological progress was the dream of development advisers, Dr Schumacher was branded as an idealistic crank and his ideas received no recognition. Nevertheless, this was not a barren period for him. His classic essay *Buddhist Economics* was one of the fruits of this experience. He realized that it was not the Third World which should learn about the high technology of the West, but rather the West which should learn from the spiritual perception of the East.

It was not until 1966 that he was able to form a small group of like-minded people to disseminate information and knowledge about intermediate technology and an indigenous form of development through self-help. In a climate of gradual disillusionment with the concept of unlimited economic growth, coupled with a growing feeling of alienation produced by a high technology society, Schumacher's ideas began to gain a slow, grass-roots acceptance. In 1973 his first book, *Small is Beautiful*, came out in Britain but met with only a lukewarm reception. It was not until the following year when the American edition was published, widely acclaimed and followed by a series of lecture tours and promotion campaigns that his ideas started to receive more serious and widespread attention both in America and Europe. However, Schumacher's ideas were still regarded as optimistic alternatives and had little effect in penetrating the planning and policies of the government. The pursuit of size, speed and growth in defiance of all laws of natural harmony still continued.

But his vision, ideas and beliefs continued to take effect. 'His influence,' as John Seymour observed, 'was in his presence which was magnificent, his character, which one can only describe as loveable, his rock-like common sense, his freshness of approach and constant probing into new realms of thought and new ideas. I don't believe anybody ever listened to him talk without coming under his spell. No matter how inimical an audience was to his ideas it could not listen to him without considering those ideas. He addressed, directly, probably tens of thousands of people in Europe and America and Australia – some of them the most influential in the world. He affected them all, every one of them.'

Schumacher's message of 'economics as if people matter' is as relevant to the West as it is to the East. He rejected the intellectual tradition of Descartes, Adam Smith and Keynes, which upholds the superiority of logical, rational objective knowledge to the detriment of all other forms. He expressed his holistic thinking, his wisdom, with such clarity and humanity, and with the weight of an experienced economist, that even those who disagreed with him could not ignore him.

Introduction

After his death in 1977, *Resurgence* magazine, of which he was an associate editor, launched the Schumacher Society to promote his vision and further his ideas – in particular, the principle of 'small is beautiful'. But, of course, not just 'small is beautiful', for small can be ugly too. The Schumacher Society was founded to promote what is beautiful as well as small. Small must be ecological, spiritual, fulfilling and harmonious. Then, and only then, can small command our attention.

I can think of no better way to show appreciation of Dr Schumacher's life and work than to publish these most original and radical lectures in which the speakers reveal not only their minds, but their hearts too. As they unite the inner and outer realities they also unite the intellect with the emotions, and that is why these lectures stand out from the dry world of pure academia.

Publishing these particular thinkers in one book is a step towards working together and introducing new ways of looking at the world; ways which do not provide a ready-made blueprint for a new society but which are indicative of a direction which we must all discover together.

Satish Kumar
Hartland,
Devon, 1980

Tribute to Schumacher

Leopold Kohr

If the Nobel Prize selection committee had wished to give the prize in economics to an innovator, they would not have alternated between the repairmen of the left and the repairmen of the right side of the ship of state caught in the increasing pull of Niagara River a mile above the Falls; they would have selected Dr E. F. Schumacher, whose death on 6 September 1977 of a heart attack in Switzerland tore him away at the very time his ideas were close to a breakthrough. He was one of the few economists who had really something new to offer. Instead of concentrating on mending the sides of the overgrown hull of the ship, he suggested: get out of it. Save yourself in a fleet of small lifeboats.

A former protégé of Maynard Keynes, who brought the young German student during the last war from internment on an isolated English farm to the fermenting halls of Oxford University, Schumacher first captured the famous economist's attention through a paper, *Multilateral Clearing*, which he had written between tending the fields. When it was published in the spring of 1943 in *Economica*, it caused some embarrassment to Keynes who, instead of arranging for its separate publication, had used the essay almost verbatim in his famous *Plan for an International Clearing Union* which the British Government issued as a White Paper a few weeks later.

In his swift rise, Schumacher became chief editorial

writer on economics for *The Times*, a Kissinger-like achievement for a native German so early in post-war England. In this capacity he was, among other things, in due course charged with the somewhat uncomfortable task of preparing, many years before the event, the obituary of Maynard Keynes, of whose theories he had by then become increasingly critical. He subsequently served as adviser to the India Planning Commission, as well as to the governments of Zambia and Burma – an experience which led to his fascinating essay on *Buddhist Economics*. The final twenty years before his retirement, he held the position of Chief Economist to the British Coal Board, and later Chief Statistician. I presume it was his attempt to penetrate the inextricable complexities confronting the overblown political and economic giant organizations of our time that gave him the first idea for writing *Small is Beautiful* which, among many other things, revealed him as the only person who had accurately and consistently predicted for fifteen years the approach of the world's current fuel crisis.

Schumacher's basic development theories can be summed up in two catch-phrases: Intermediate Size, and Intermediate Technology.

About the first, he wrote:

A given political unity is not necessarily of the right size as a unit for economic development . . . In this matter [of appropriate size] it is not possible to give hard and fast definitions. Much depends on geography and local circumstances. A few thousand people, no doubt, would be too few to constitute a 'district' for economic development. But the community of a few hundred thousand people, even if fairly widely scattered, may well deserve to be created as a development district. The whole of Switzerland has less than 6 million inhabitants. Yet it is divided into more than 20 cantons and each canton is a kind of [autonomous] development district, with the result that development towards formation of vast industrial concentration is minimized.

In other words, the first half of Schumacher's development philosophy is based on the administrative idea of superimposing on large-area states a cantonal structure of such modest unit-dimensions that vast industrial concentration (with all this entails in imbalance, ineptitude, and diseconomies of scale) becomes not only unnecessary but also uneconomical.

The second half of his system – Intermediate Technology – is the direct consequence of the first. For once a development district is 'appropriately' reduced, it becomes possible to fulfil a society's material requirements by means of less expensive and simpler equipment than the costly, computerized, labour-saving machinery necessary for satisfying the massive appetite for the remedial transport and integration commodities without which a far-flung modern market community cannot exist. Though this means a reduction in productivity, it does not mean a reduction in the product that a smaller society needs for the enjoyment of even the highest humanely attainable standard of living.

Putting it differently, the reduced efficiency of *intermediate* technology provides the same amount of goods, but at a higher cost in labour, than can be achieved under conditions of labour-saving *advanced* technology. However, since higher labour cost (in terms not of wages but of longer working hours) means simply that the desired level of production can be achieved only by full rather than partial employment of the available labour force, they represent *socially* no additional cost at all. They are, in fact, a benefit. It is unemployment – the degrading saving of manpower through the inappropriate use of advanced machinery – which is the prohibitive cost which no society can afford to pay in the long run. For unlike earlier forms of unemployment, the unemployment caused by excessive technological progress spells in the end only one thing – the revolt of the unemployed.

This is still only vaguely understood by modern growth theorists for whom intermediate technology means merely a step backwards. One has to go back all the way to Vespasian to encounter a government advanced enough to realize the social value of higher rather than lower costs. As Suetonius tells us: When an inventor offered the Emperor to transport giant columns to the top of Capitol hill at an unheard-of low cost, Vespasian rewarded him richly for his technical genius, but dispensed with his services with the remark, 'You must permit me also to let the man in the street earn his bread.' By the standards of modern economics, this would earn a student a failing grade at Harvard or Oxford.

Lately, however, with orthodox economics having run its course, and hiding its ineptitudes in mathematical obscurity of Nobel-Prize-winning proportions, Schumacher's ideas, particularly on the question of how to sponge up unemployment and at the same time solve the energy crisis, have begun to make their impact in Asian and African countries whose leaders realize that what is needed is not highfalutin theory but a bit of horse sense. People such as Indians, or Zambians, and lately even leaders such as Governor Brown of California and President Carter of the United States (though not yet the economists advising them) seem to be among the first since Vespasian to understand once again after their talks with Schumacher that *New* Man, whose coming they all await with such impatience, is in need of two props: an *older* mode of production in the form of *intermediate technology*, and an *older* political environment in the form of more translucent, smaller and more meaningfully human societies.

There was also another side to Schumacher's praise of smallness of which few of his admirers were aware. This had to do neither with technology nor with political organization, but with the composition of delightful verses for his children. I was fortunate to acquire some of them when, after a week's stay as my guest in Puerto Rico in 1973, I somewhat shocked him with the request to sign a paper in order to balance his accounts with me. He laughed when he found out that what I wanted was not a promissory note, but the text in his own handwriting of the poem he had recited to me earlier that day – and which I should like to share with the reader in memory of a friend who inspired us all not only by his wisdom and charm, but also by the abiding humour of his humanity.

> Little children, surely,
> Age you prematurely.
> Though, if all be told:
> They keep you young when old.

THE SCHUMACHER LECTURES

Edited by Satish Kumar

I
What is the Matter with Mind?

R. D. Laing

Surely it is obvious enough if one looks at the whole world that it is becoming daily better cultivated and more fully peopled than anciently. All places are now accessible, all are well known, all open to commerce. Most pleasant farms have obliterated all traces of what were once dreary and dangerous wastes. Cultivated fields have subdued forests. Flocks and herds have expelled wild beasts. Sandy deserts are sown, rocks are planted, marshes are drained and where once were hardly solitary cottages there are now large cities. No longer are islands dreaded nor their rocky shores feared, everywhere are houses and inhabitants and settled government and civilized life. Our teaming population is the strongest evidence, our numbers are burdensome to the world which can hardly support us from its natural elements, our wants grow more and more keen and our complaints more bitter in all mouths whilst nature fails in affording us our usual sustenance. In every deed pestilence and famine and wars and earthquakes have to be regarded as a remedy for nations, as the means of pruning the luxuriance of the human race.

Thus wrote Tertullian in his *Treatise on the Soul*, AD 210 (quoted by Stevenson (1957) p.189). Whatever we are into has been going on for many generations. Is it all right? Did something happen? Is anything the matter?

1

R. D. Laing

I

As far as I have heard, no other species is known to have changed its ways of being on this planet so quickly as large sections of the human species have done in barely the last two thousand years of human history.

The process must have been going on for some time before the above could have been written.

Remember Plutarch's story of that wail that rose from the island of Paladese, when the pilot Thamose announced across the waters from the stern of the ship: 'Great Pan is dead.' Those lamentations and cries of amazement wafted themselves even to Tiberius Caesar, we are told, and they are still wafting themselves down to us today.

> We have lost Abraxas, the terrible and beautiful god of both day and night in Gnosticism. We have lost totemism, the sense of parallelism between man's organization and that of the animals and plants. We have lost even the Dying God.
>
> (Bateson p.19)

Maybe something may have happened. Something may be the matter.

Let us ponder with thoughtful men over these matters, and in so doing try to look at the way we look at them, for whatever we think we should be doing depends on what the situation looks like. The explanation needs a description to explain.

Many of us feel a great unease about various aspects of the subtopia that human minds and hands have created, the world of man-made artifacts, the world that Karl Popper and Eccles have recently been calling World 3, the world of the material externalization of ourselves. A number of those who have pondered on why this is so have diagnosed the situation as a dis-

2

order, a dislocation between man and his environment, and have suggested that this dislocation, this alienation is perhaps a reflection of a spiritual-intellectual *malaise* which expresses itself in deep intellectual confusion. Amusingly enough, one man's confusion is another's clarity.

Schumacher (1978), Bateson (1979), Monod (1974) and C. S. Lewis (1978) are among a host of others who have tried to describe those trends in the Western mind which seem to them to be out of step, or out of key, dis-attuned, to the nature of the universe – a disjunctive relation, they all agree, which seems to manifest itself both as epistemological errors and as malpractice towards our one and only life support system, the world. But there is diametric disagreement as to what is the matter. Indeed, each side epitomizes what is the matter to the other. In either case, these trends are not identified as loose ends around the margins of contemporary thought and practice, but are found in the mainstream of successful scientific, technological, educational and political endeavour.

We cannot fashion an explanatory silk purse out of a descriptive sow's ear. What we see is a unity of how we look and what we see. How does it look *biologically*, for instance?

Whitehead, among many others, has warned us against espousing the view that there is an essential bifurcation of nature into mind and matter.

We fit or we do not fit our environmental life-support system. If our genetic keys fit the environmental lock, we open the door to survival, at any rate to the next round of life. The survivors are those who fit their ecological niche. We are here because we have survived. We have survived because the powers that be so far have not deigned to destroy us.

The ultimate elements of our being are, as far as has

3

been ascertained, of exactly the same stuff as everything else. In us, this material is arranged in patterns which have a limited persistence. A genetic pattern which we call a species seems to persist through a few million years.

The biological tautology is that we are survivors because we fit best, and we fit best because we have survived. Yet, 'we' do not survive. A material *form* survives which we call a species.

II

All species have a species life. The species is not immortal either. We have no warrant of any kind to suppose that the human species has any special privilege to escape extinction. Many of us are more upset about the thought that some day there will be no human beings at all than about the thought that you and I are going to die. But shall it be a healthy death in a healthy old age? Or shall we kill ourselves directly or indirectly?

We are transforms of materia, patterns of ultra-microscopic dust. From dust to dust, the patterns that survive are those which best fit into the patterns we are. The most exquisitely perfect adaptation must be adaption to the pattern which connects all patterns.

It is no use asking what pattern is *that*, but it is, at any rate, clear that the patterns in the dust are not themselves dust. A pattern of pipes is not a pipe. A pattern of dust is not dust. No painting without paint, although the painting is not the paint.

We are mental matter, material minds. To say, on the other hand, that matter *is* mind, is like saying a television set is the programme it is showing. A lot of so-called organic or biological psychiatry is a theory and practice based on the same sort of epistemological error implied by calling in a TV technician to tinker with a TV set because one does not like the programme. Without the hardware there would be no programme. Without the programme there would be no *point* in the hardware.

I ask my mind: What is your habitat? What or where or when do you feel at home?

My mind replies: Whenever I find information in matter of the spirit's information of matter I feel happier, comforted, at home.

What is the ecology of mind, in the biological scheme of things?

III

> Flower in the crannied wall,
> I pluck you out of the crannies.

Tennyson plucks out that flower without hesitation, and with no misgivings.

> I hold you here, root and all, in my hand,
> Little flower – but if I could understand
> What you are, root and all, and all in all,
> I should know what God and man is.

Ah! But if only!

The flower I hold in my hand is plucked out root and all from all in all.

Maybe the impulse to pluck, the sense of a perfect right to pluck, and the act of plucking already comprise and imply such ignorance of what God and man is, that nothing but progress and advancement in the path of error can be predicted from there on in.

It is easier to put back that plucked flower I hold in my hand than to put the ontological, poetic, metaphoric, existential flower back in its ontological, poetic, metaphoric, existential crannie.

It goes without saying, it is tedious even to mention, that the flower has to be plucked to be held in my hand. There is a way of seeing that flower-in-the crannied-wall as something-in-my-hand.

We have plucked a lot of flowers. And kept on plucking plucks off the plucks back to the dust until the pattern disappears in where it appears from.

IV

Bearing in mind with caution Whitehead's ontological warning against the view of an *essential* bifurcation in what is, empirically, ontically different, we do seem to be confronted by a reality that presents itself to us in two widely different ways. First, as *experience*. The reality of our experience, the reality we know directly, the *only* form of reality we know directly. Experience presents itself to us in a repertoire of varieties, or versions – as sensations, perceptions, cognitions, feelings, intentions, desires and aversions, as convictions, imagination, memory, visions, hallucinations, as ineffable states of rapture, absorption, ecstasy and bliss.

Secondly, whatever it is that is, presents itself to us as a reality which is beyond our experience; a reality which is *essentially* non-experiential, a reality upon which our experience seems to feed, of which some believe our experience to be at best a transform, perhaps a shadow.

Our subjectivity cannot be seen, touched. It is not an object. It exists, and yet the immediacy of our existence is closed to, is not available for, is inaccessible to natural scientific study.

We know that meaning, value, quality, love and hate, good and evil, beauty and ugliness, exist in some sort of way, which is not a number or quantity, or a thing. We know, therefore, that we, our existing selves, are immeasurable. Job's balances are not to be found in a physicist's laboratory.

The natural scientist explicitly excludes that subjective morass, he leaves all that behind, he sheds all he can of it, before even embarking on his voyage of scientific discovery.

And the scientist returns, Jacques Monod tells us, loaded with his treasures and power which he offers to men, and, yes, *they* grab them, *they* avidly consume them. But, he goes on, they have scarcely even heard the 'profounder message' of science, which is 'a new and unique source of truth'. We are living by values 'blasted at the root by science itself'.

> No society before ours was ever torn apart by such conflicts. In both primitive and classical cultures the animist tradition saw knowledge and values stemming from the same source. For the first time in history a civilization is trying to shape itself while clinging desperately to the animist tradition in an effort to justify its values, and at the same time abandoning it as the source of knowledge, of truth.

According to Monod, there is a sickness of the modern spirit, a lie at the root of man's moral and social nature, an ailment, more or less confusedly diagnosed,

> That provokes the fear if not the hatred – in any case the estrangement – felt toward scientific culture by so many people today. Their aversion, when openly expressed, is usually directed at the technological by-products of science: the bomb, the destruction of nature, the soaring population. It is easy, of course, to answer that technology and science are not the same thing, and moreover that the use of atomic energy will soon be vital to mankind's survival; that the destruction of nature denotes a faulty technology rather than too much of it; and that the

7

population soars because millions of children are saved from death every year. Are we to go back to letting them die?

Behind this protest, Monod tells us, lurks

> The refusal to accept the essential message of science. The fear is the fear of sacrilege: of outrage to values; and it is wholly justified. It is perfectly true that science attacks values. Not directly, since science is no judge of them and must ignore them . . .

> . . . If he accepts this message in its full significance, man must at last wake out of his millenary dream and discover his total solitude, his fundamental isolation. He must realize that, like a gypsy, he lives on the boundary of an alien world; a world that is deaf to his music, and as indifferent to his hopes as it is to his suffering or his crimes.
> (Monod (1974) p.159–161)

> Ethics, in essence *nonobjective*, is for ever barred from the sphere of knowledge.
> (Monod, op.cit. p.162)

No echo of the wails and lamentations of a long lost 'animism', no regrets, no sentimental, romantic, decadent, soft-minded corruption by the ghost of the pathetic fallacy for Jacques Monod. To him, all this is sick nostalgia, a blight on the human spirit. Although he does not speak for every natural scientist, by any means, I want to use him to characterize a type of mind.

V

The starting-point for science is an already sophisticated transform of naive experience. But science does not stay within its initially already objectified, quantified, de-experientialized experience. It goes beyond all experience, however experientially ablated, which remains its starting- and returning-point, to explain it, to predict it, and so the better to manipulate and change it, to control it, to try to destroy it, maybe, who knows, to create it. The scientist 'explains' the realities or fictions of experience from inferred non-experientable events, real or fictional, and he tests the reliability and validity of his real *explanans* by reference to his unreal *explananda*.

In order to begin to be a scientist, the pre-scientist, the prospective scientist has to perform a number of entirely subjective operations on his own subjectivity. These entail an attempted de-subjectification and objectification of his scientific domain. This requires (1) the ablation or elimination of some or all sense data; (2) the temporary suspension of any subject of cognizance; (3) the cutting off of any relation of intersubjectivity, or interiority; (4) the de-realization of any subjectivity out there.

It is paradoxical that this de-subjectification and objectification is such a subjective act. What on earth happens to our *sense* of reality, which is nothing if not subjective, in the face of the suspension, the ablation, the attempted total elimination, of our subjectivity which *includes* our very sense of reality, with all the realities that depend on it and upon which depend all feeling, all quality, all value? Erasure of subjectivity, in order to be objective, is itself a subjective act. What else can it be? The self-desubjectified-objectified scientist in a de-subjectified-objectified world is already experiencing an altered reality, he is looking at altered reality in an altered way. Science originally is a way of seeing.

It seems to me that the mind must already be dis-affected from ordinary everyday reality, before it can be stirred to find ways and means to annihilate it.

VI

Democritus is among the first on record to have started to prepare the ground for science by a proper sense of the unreality of ordinary reality. In those celebrated fragments he tells us that we must learn that we are 'severed from *reality*' (Diels fr.6). Colour, bitter and sweet, that is (we are, I think, entitled to presume), the *sense* of colour, of taste, are contingent conventions (fr.9,11,125). We can know nothing in *reality*, but only a transform of reality, the product of an impingement upon our fickle sensors from a reality we can infer, but never know through direct experience.

> There are two sorts of knowledge, one genuine, one bastard. To the latter belong all the following: sight, hearing, smell, taste, touch. The *real* is separated from this. When the bastard can do no more – neither see more minutely, nor hear, nor smell, nor taste, nor perceive by touch – and a finer investigation is needed, then the genuine comes in as having a tool for distinguishing more finely.
>
> (trans. Freeman (1956) p.93)

Nevertheless, our senses (including our common sense) reply:

> Wretched intellect. You get your evidence from us, and you try to overthrow us? Your victory is your defeat.
>
> (Diels, fr.125)

Sight, sound, taste, touch and smell, and later into the same bracket with our senses, all sensibility, all values,

10

all quality, all feelings, all motives, all intentions, spirit, soul, consciousness, subjectivity: almost everything, in fact, which we ordinarily take to be real is *de*-realized, is stripped of its pretensions to reality. What is *evident*, phenomena, of all kinds, as such, are all bastards. The phenomenal world is no longer self-evident. It is not *real*. It is not genuine; it is false. It is a copy, a shadow, a counterfeit, a sign of, a map of, an index of that which occasions it. But this bastard is our jailer. How shall we escape from his clutches?

At the least, we have begun to experience an urge to go beyond it, to account for it, or perhaps not even to account for it, but to find out something of what seems to be *really* going on, behind it, beyond it, *in* it. From this vertex, we are interested in 'real' phenomena only in so far as they can help us to get to those imputed transcendental goings on that for ever mock the necessary contingencies of our immanence.

This de-realization of ordinary reality is no mere matter of stripping off a veneer of appearance. It entails a profound transformation of our whole being in the world. Most amazingly and paradoxically, in our journey into objectivity and beyond, it is by acts of pure subjectivity that we have to divest ourselves of our subjectivity.

The Democritian step was taken over 2,000 years ago, but it has to be repeated every time we get our minds into the vertex of an objective scientific probe of outside phenomena. This is the vertex of Galileo and Newton, in contrast to Giordano Bruno and Goethe. Galileo's reality is objective. It remains true, whether he denies it or not. It is independent of him. He can deny it without denying himself. But in order to achieve this reciprocal independence of the subjective self and *objective* reality, one has, in a sense, to cut out the subjective *from* reality, and in so doing

11

precisely to cut our subjectivity off from the objective and objectified world, in pain of committing the pathetic fallacy.

Galileo's celebrated *Denken Experiment* calls for the subjective ablation of irrelevant or inconvenient subjective reality.

> Now I say that whenever I conceive any material or corporeal substance, I immediately feel the need to think of it as bounded, and as having this or that shape; as being large or small in relation to other things, and in some specific place at any given time; as being in motion or at rest; as touching or not touching some other body; and as being one in number, or few, or many. From these conditions I cannot separate such a substance by any stretch of my imagination. But that it must be white or red, bitter or sweet, noisy or silent, and of sweet or foul odor, my mind does not feel compelled to bring in as necessary accompaniments. Without the senses as our guides, reason or imagination unaided would probably never arrive at qualities like these. Hence I think that tastes, odor, colours, and so on are no more than mere names so far as the object in which we place them is concerned, and that they reside only in the consciousness. Hence if the living creatures were removed, all these qualities would be wiped away and annihilated. But since we have imposed upon them special names, distinct from those of the other and real qualities mentioned previously, we wish to believe that they really exist as actually different from those.

> (trans. Drake (1957) p.272)

Such thought-experiments have been undertaken by intellectuals, mystics, metaphysicians, speculative and analytic philosophers. But the scientist does not eliminate himself and his sense data like the meditator, concentrating on an unseen point, until all content, name and form evaporate. He goes beyond the phenomena, he discards them, but he handles them to go through them, he attacks them, mucks around with them, manipulates them, changes them, predicts them, *controls* them if he can.

It will be a matter not only of nature

> Free and large (when she is left to her own course and does her work her own way) – such as that of the heavenly bodies, meteors, earth and sea, minerals, plants, animals – but much more of nature under constraint and vexed; that is to say, when by art and the hand of man she is forced out of her natural state, and squeezed and moulded.
>
> (Bacon (1960) p.25)

One has to feel very free to handle Mother Nature, the Earth Goddess herself, and the veritable personal handwork of God Himself, in so ruthless a fashion. But science has ablated subjectivity, hence values. Things have no value in themselves, the only scientific terms of reference are scientific.

> Some are weakly afraid lest a deeper search into nature should transgress the permitted limits of sober-mindedness, wrongfully wresting and transferring what is said in Holy Writ against those who pry into sacred mysteries, to the hidden things of nature, *which are barred by no prohibition.* (my italics)
>
> (Bacon, op.cit. p.88)

The decision to jettison the ethical and compassion in order to pursue scientific work untrammelled, unbridled by any merely 'subjective' considerations is, inescapably, a pre-scientific, or metascientific ethical decision, and an act of subjectivity itself. The scientist decides, implicitly or explicitly, that he is doing nothing *he* regards as ethically or scientifically wrong by elim-

13

inating ethics from scientific evidence in theory and practice. He may limit his scientific probes to domains he finds ethically inoffensive, but the same scientific procedures applied to humans, as applied to rats, mice, dogs, monkeys or any other experimental animal, would be no less scientific for being ethically abhorrent.

Needham gives this as a rare early example of 'a serious discussion of scientific method, and the planning of the experiment'.

At the time of the first publication of the present work, my friend Dr. R. W. Gerard brought to my notice a curious story, the origin of which he was unable to trace, that Cleopatra, the Ptolemaic queen, had investigated the process of foetal development by the dissection of slaves at known intervals of time from conception, following the precepts of Hippocrates with regard to hen's eggs. The story is, it seems, Rabbinic (cf. Preuss, p.451). R. Ismael (Nidd. III. 7) taught that the male foetus was complete in 41, the female in 81, days, and cited as his authority the results of the above Alexandrian experiment. Sceptics urged that copulation might have taken place before the experiment began, but supporters replied that an abortifacient was, of course, given. Sceptics begged leave to doubt the universal efficiency of these drugs. They also questioned whether intercourse between the slaves and the prison guards had been absolutely guarded against.

(Needham (1959) p.65)

The Good and the True, value and knowledge parted company a long time ago. Does such profound division *of* reality, reflect our essential bifurcation *in* reality?

VI

The value of the object is not an object. Since values have no objective existence, and objective existence is the domain of natural science, science does not study the value of existence. It studies the existence that is valuable.

What is scientifically right may be ethically wrong.

VII

Objective science, being non-subjective, has nothing to say about knowledge of subjectivity, about the knowing subject and his relation to other known subjects. Our intersubjectivity, our hopes, our fears, our promises, our oaths, our intentions, our betrayals, our faith, our belief, our hate and our love, our sense of right and wrong – all our subjective values are objectively valueless. Perception, Merleau-Ponty used to claim, was an act of communion. This communion is not part of the scientific method and is scientifically, objectively, epistemologically worthless.

Without it, however, there is no mediation between the world and the scientist whereby the world could have a meaning-for-him. For, as Schrödinger (op.cit.) says:

> The show that is going on obviously acquires a meaning only with regard to the mind that contemplates it. But what science tells us about this relationship is patently absurd: as if mind had only been produced by that very display that it is now watching and would pass away with it when the sun finally cools down and the earth has been turned into a desert of ice and snow.'
>
> (Schrödinger (1977) p.149)

Monod's essential message of science is patently absurd to Schrödinger. Be that as it may, it is evident that Monod's essential message of objective science is a fully fashioned subjective construction placed on his subjectively objectified scientific experience.

I think that somewhere along the Western, Sumerian–Babylonian, Egyptian, Judaeo-Christian line, we (a lot of us) lost the *experience* of a bond between our experience and the universe of which it is a part, not apart. The tattered remnant of this bond is called 'animism' by Jacques Monod, the persistence of which he regards as mankind's biggest hang-up and hangover from his pre-scientific epochs of Ur-stupidity.

The Bacon–Monodian scientific stance extols vexing, tormenting, torturing the secrets out of nature, extols knowing the truth of nature stripped of our experience of her or it. It recommends its manipulation, control. It connives at its exploitation and destruction. All this is not only allowable, not only barred by no prohibition, but gleefully and avidly pursued with self-congratulatory encomiums with the reckless abandon of extreme spiritual depravity.

VIII

The scientist discards values, by his own declaration. Perhaps he is entitled to do so, but then to tell us poor animists that our values are valueless, as far as knowledge and truth are concerned, is as sensible as a man who has blinded himself telling the rest of us that what we think we see are only hallucinations, if anything.

IX

Let us consider the issue of *quality*. Consider music. Its phenomenal elements are punctate notes, of definite assigned pitch. To the person with perfect pitch each note has its own special quality, which is not the same experience as the sheer quantitative pitch of the note.

Even for those who do not have perfect pitch, in a tune each note acquires a special quality, which is a property of the sonic system of which the tune is a part. The quality of a part is a property of the system of which it is a part. The most detailed analysis of each note separately will not begin to help us to infer a melody, unless we have heard a melody.

But a melody is not made up only of notes. It is made of the relations (of pitch, of time, of timbre, of loudness and softness) between them. The interval between two notes is not itself a note. A melody is the phenomenalization of an entirely abstract and formal set of relations, silent relations. The sound delineates or shapes the silence.

As in information theory, we are concerned with news of difference. The difference between two notes is not a note, as the difference between two phonemes is not a phoneme. The relations between two or more people are not themselves persons. The relation between man and his environment is there anyway, inescapably, all the time, although it cannot be *found* by us anywhere else than in the *experience* of that relation. The *melody* cannot be studied if the relations between the notes which comprise it are not heard as a melody.

Let those who cannot hear melodies not tell us that melodies do not exist because they do not hear them. Nor let those who hear melodies be intimidated into believing that the actual immediate experience of *quality*, musical or in any other domain, has no epistemological relevance. I may *infer* a wine is of good quality, by a quantitative analysis of its definable and measurable ingredients, but I only *know* if it is or not by its bouquet and taste.

In international economic plans, *bread* is quantified as so much flour, carbohydrates and so on – and costed accordingly. However, no account as far as I am told is taken of the *quality* of the bread in question, its texture and taste in the mouth, its softness or crispness; that is, no account is taken of how *well* it is *baked*, and the state it is in by the time it gets to the consumer's mouth, sliced, wrapped, deep-frozen, or smelling deliciously straight out of the bakery.

Surely this is absurd. It would be as though one assessed the merits of a piece of music by counting the mix of the notes, or judged a novel by the percentages of parts of speech, or assessed a good wine by its percentage of ethyl alcohol and other ingredients.

Not only has *bread as such* disappeared from the plan, leaving only a collection of molecules, but the context of the bread (bakery – local shop; bread factory – a thousand supermarkets) is also missing. And yet surely it is the *quality* of life which is the object of the whole exercise.

Without being orientated to that end, planning is orientated by a component (quantification) of a means to an end (quality). A means has usurped its place and become the one sole means and its own sole end.

Why are we doing ourselves in in this way?

X

All natural science can say about values is that they do not come within its *domain of investigative competence*.

A few of the other modes of existence outside the investigative competence of natural science, besides value, are love and hate, joy and sorrow, misery and happiness, pleasure and pain, right and wrong, purpose, meaning, hope, courage, despair, God, heaven and hell, grace, sin, salvation, damnation, enlighten-

ment, wisdom, compassion, evil, envy, malice, gene-
rosity, camaraderie and everything, in fact, that makes
life worth living.

The natural scientist finds none of these things, and
comes back to pronounce the most obviously banal
forgone conclusions, of which he has the impertinence
to try to dragoon us into believing is the essential
message of science: *you cannot buy a camel in a donkey
market*.

Postscript

I was having a conversation recently with Fritjof Capra, the physicist and author of *The Tao of Physics*, in the course of which I asked him what he thought of Jacques Monod's *Chance and Necessity*.

His reply was to tell me that he had asked Heisenberg what *he* thought of Monod, and Heisenberg had replied, 'I don't think he really understands quantum physics.' Although I have only the faintest and vaguest of ideas what that remark implies, I somehow felt an almost imperceptible wave of no doubt quite unjustifiable relief sweep over me.

Bibliography

BATESON, G. *Mind and Nature*. London, 1979. Wildwood House.

GALILEO, G. *Discoveries and Opinions of Galileo* (ed. and trans. by S. Drake) Garden City, New York, 1957. Doubleday.

LEWIS, C. S. *The Abolition of Man*. Glasgow, 1978. Fount Paperbacks.

MONOD, J. *Chance and Necessity*. England, 1974. Collins Fontana Books.

SCHUMACHER, E. F. *A Guide for the Perplexed*. London, 1978. Abacus/Sphere Books.

SCHRÖDINGER, E. *What is Life?* Cambridge, 1977. Cambridge University Press.

STEVENSON, F. *A New Eusebius*. London, 1975. Camelot Press.

Discussion

What should I do?

I'll give you what I take to be a golden rule for me and give you a brief example as to how it operates in practice in some of the professional company I keep. *'Do to others what you would like them to do to you if you were in the other person's position.'*

Take a very simple example: In North America, Canada, New Zealand and in a large part of Europe, when a woman is about to have a baby she's put on her back with her legs up – in America in some places her ankles are put in ankle-straps and her wrists are put in wrist-straps so she's strapped up. A male obstetrician will say, 'Well, its very difficult to imagine what it must be like to be having a baby, but maybe the nearest a man can get to this thought of something coming through the perireum, the pelvic floor, is having a shit.' Now, we don't want to debase the experience of childbirth to having a shit, but nevertheless it's got a mechanical similarity in that an object is actually going through the pelvic floor. So, I say to these characters who are doing this day in and day out, 'If you were having a shit would you get down on your back and put your legs up? Just try to have a shit in that position, let alone having a baby'

Just a couple of weeks ago I was talking to a few medical students and I said that to them. One of them said, 'But how can we examine the patient then?' So you've got to spell it out further than that. 'When you feel it's necessary to examine the patient, you ask her nicely to lie down and put her legs up and let you examine her – that takes about two minutes. When that's over you let her get up again.' That guy then said to me, 'Why didn't I think of that before?' I said, 'Well, brother, you seriously ask yourself that question. You're on the edge just now, in a few months' or a few years' time, if you're like the majority of people who have gone ahead of you down into that black hole of medicine, you will not be able even to ask of yourself, "Why haven't I thought of that before?" You asked very seriously why you haven't asked that question before, and thank God that you *are* now asking it.'

St Anselm was written a letter by the Abbot of a monastery who said: 'I don't know what to do with these boys in the monastery' – in those days boys were sent to monasteries to be educated or simply to be brought up, like public schools and so forth, and many children were brought up in monasteries – 'I've been beating them black and blue, and I still can't control them. My arms are falling off with exhaustion. What am I to do?' And Anselm in a famous letter replied to him, 'Why don't you try to imagine what you would feel like if you were one of the boys and treat them in the way you would like them to treat you, if you were in their position.' That reciprocity of perspective, a cultivation, I think: we all have it to some extent but we can lose it by neglect.

R. D. Laing

What about the animals?

When William James says in his *Principles of Psychology* that we're going to study the mind, he says the first thing to do – he's talking about the human mind – is to get a frog and kill it, then cut it up and look at the different twitches of its muscles when you stimulate bits of nerves to produce twitches. Exactly as Charles Sherrington did – took Shetland ponies, cut them up into bits and studied how the bits twitched, and then tried to work out how all these twitches integrate or are integrated. Of course, these twitches never exist in a live animal. They're twitches that bits of dead flesh make when cut off from live animals. If you want to know what my finger is, what my hand is, or what my arm is, I hope you won't cut off my hand to try to find out what it is. What it is, if anything, will be my phantom arm – the hand will be left in relationship to the context from which it's been taken. But that's not what you're studying. You're studying a bit of dead flesh, not my living hand. You get all these bits of dead flesh that still twitch and then imagine how you're going to put them together and how they all cohere.

The error which I think vitiates mechanistic biology surfaces in terms of behaviour modification. There is a certain sort of complex device called an animal, called a human being, to which we do various things to get it to do this if we do that, and so forth. While we plough ourselves into this way of looking at things we're not hearing the melody, we're simply cracking up some of its single notes: there's no melody there. And when there isn't any melody left we haven't suffered any sense of loss, because we've gone deaf to the melody long before it has, in fact, disappeared. The dreadful has already happened, long before we dot the 'i's' and stroke the 't's'. It is, as Heidigger said, so technologically sweet to carry out these procedures once we can, but when we look at them in a certain way, not only do we have to do them in that way, we are no longer able to imagine any other way of doing them.

What can we do when other people oppress us?

There is a sense of fairness in the principle 'live and let live'. I'm not going to do to you something that I would find objectionable for you to do to me. At the same time, I'm not going to let you do to me what I don't want done to me. I'm not going to let you wipe me out. If you treat me in a way that I feel is unreasonable, then I shall respond to you in a way that you won't like and I shall continue until you desist from treating me in that manner. Well, some of you might feel that that's going too far in terms of belligerence, but that's the sort of guy I am. I feel perfectly entitled to stand up for myself and not let anyone do me into the ground.

I certainly don't feel that it does the other person any good to let them use me as a doormat, anymore than it does me any good to do that to the other person, anymore than it does the other person any good to have that done to them. So, we have to stand up for ourselves. It's a reciprocity; thou shalt not trespass. 'Forgive us our trespasses, as we forgive them that trespass against us.' Well, I'm prepared to forgive a trespass but not to forget it; I forgive you but don't try it again. That's not revenge, although very likely there will be a bit of revenge in it. But let's live, and let's let live.

We have to put ourselves in someone else's position – accept their perspective, their reality and their world as long as these do not trespass in turn on anyone else's. A false argument along these lines is used very frequently in institutionalized medicine in this country where it has now become general practice not to tell someone that they are dying when it is known that they are dying. The people who are implementing this policy will say, 'Well, if I was dying I wouldn't like to know.' That's not good enough.

Is the family a pathological institution?

In advanced technological societies the family has very often been reduced to a nuclear family. Sometimes it consists only of a husband and wife, and frequently the family is mobile. It is not embedded in a network of familial and other relationships, such as in a Levi Strauss Kinship Chart where there are as many as seventy nominated kinship relationships, all organized like a crystal around each person. Our nuclear family is just a little fragment of what is the anthropological family norm. The two parents rely on each other for practically everything – economic, emotional, sexual and moral support and re-sustenance of energy. Both parents may go off to different places in the course of twenty-four hours, leaving the children in the hands of strangers. It is a very unusual system; in fact, as far as I know, it is one of the new nuances this century has produced. It puts extraordinary strain and stress on the members of such a situation. I've tried to document some of the secondary consequences of the type of strain and stress that happens in such circumstances, but I hope not with a view to annulling the family, nor proposing that we should by some form of human engineering and state planning abolish families altogether, as has almost happened in some places. I rather hope we can reconstitute the family as a less fraught and more stable and happy place to be.

In some quarters, the family seems to be evaporating. An American Professor of Sociology told me recently that in America the courts have the problem of who gets custody of the child when the parents have separated. Nowadays, neither party may want custody of the child and the judge has to decide what to do – the bond between the parents, and between them and the child, has evaporated. That's the kind of thing I find saddening, because I feel it is important for children to grow up, as I did, in the context of their own family. The family is still a social form I cherish.

II
Soft Energy Paths

Amory Lovins

About the time I was first learning of the ideas of Fritz Schumacher, whose life and work we have the honour here to celebrate, I heard the story of an American woman living in India who called in a carpenter to fix a window-frame. She gave the carpenter a sketch but he followed the sketch too literally and botched the job. When she remonstrated, saying, 'Why didn't you just use your common sense?', he drew himself up with great dignity and said, 'But common sense, Madam, is a gift of God; I have technical knowledge only.'

'Technical knowledge only' seemed a good epitaph for a civilization which had not yet learned that engineering economics cannot be the sole basis of a humane public policy, nor, indeed, is it as important a criterion as social and moral values. But this view, rising from our native common sense and reinforced by such object-lessons as Concorde, is now seeping through the cracks of political consciousness. We no longer accept so uncritically the dogma that whatever we are technically able to do is worth doing – or, as Francis Bacon put it, 'The End of our Foundation is the knowledge of Causes, the secret motions of things; and the enlarging of the bounds of Human Empire, to the effecting of all things possible.' All things possible are becoming too expensive and too dangerous for us not to be more discriminating.

As this technological imperative also loses its mythic

power, we are starting to appreciate anew the wisdom of Ecclesiastes 5: 'He that hath silver shall not be satisfied with silver; nor he that hath abundance with increase: this is also vanity.' We are learning that our success in swelling and speeding the flow of goods and services (and their accompanying ills and nuisances and radical monopolies) does not mean we are achieving human satisfaction or joy or inward growth; and that an economy driven by greed, avarice, envy, gluttony, luxury and pride – in fact, all the Seven Deadly Sins, as Lewis Mumford reminds us, except sloth – such an economy is incapable of working that inner transformation for which our cultural tradition urges us to strive.

This pervasive reappraisal of means and ends has found its way into the energy debate – perhaps the central policy issue of our time. Three years ago at the nuclear research centre in Tennessee I saw someone wearing a lapel button which said: 'Technology is the ANSWER!' (But what was the question?) Yet this embarrassingly eloquent message was not as out of place at Oak Ridge as one might suppose, because defining the question – a task whose importance Fritz showed us with luminous clarity – is also, after all, the starting-point of all good engineering. Indeed, central to his essay on Buddhist economics is the classical engineering criterion of economy of means. It is for this reason, as I shall try to show, that in energy policy, if one follows the basic tenets of Buddhist economics, then Western economics will take care of itself.

In the United States, Congressman Mo Udall recently reported seeing by the roadside in Southern California a large hoarding, a billboard, which said: 'YE SHALL PAY FOR YOUR SINS!' – 2 Corinthians something or other – under which somebody had written: 'Ye who have already paid, please disregard this notice.' Well, in energy policy we have not paid yet. A glut of cheap oil has almost ruined us because we were thinking only of the short term, but we are learning belatedly how to do better by using our common sense. With your indulgence, then, and in the spirit of Fritz's contagious concern for that long term in which, I hope, we shall not all be dead, I should like to take energy as my text to help you to explore a hopeful view of our resource and social problems – a view on which I have found many people converging as I run around the energy grapevine in about fifteen countries and cross-pollinate.

To outline this convergence, I should like to sketch two hypothetical and illustrative paths along which our energy system might evolve over the next fifty years. These paths are not meant as precise forecasts or recommendations. Although I think they are technically realistic, they are meant rather as a qualitative vehicle for ideas. I am going to use a mixture of British and American examples, but I do not intend that to be restrictive, because studies on these lines are done or are being done in about fifty places around the world, and the results already in show very clearly that, with due variation of technical details from one place to another, the same principles apply essentially anywhere.

I shall select from a wide range of material. The basic thesis is set out in the 1977 Pelican book *Soft Energy Paths*: *Toward a Durable Peace*, and if you really want to dig into the literature, a couple of US Senate Committees (Small Business and Interior) have put out a nice paperweight, *Alternative Long-Range Energy Strategies* (2 vols. USGPO 1978), containing all but the latest three of the 36 or so published critiques of my work, with responses. There are also some more recent technical papers. Because all of these are available, I should like to resist until our discussion the temptation to get into the more seductive technical details and to concentrate instead on some fundamental concepts.

Until two or three years ago there was a strong industry–government consensus – remnants of which still linger – a consensus throughout the industrial world, that the energy future should be like the past only more so, and that the energy problem is simply where to get more domestic energy to meet extrapolated demands. But the demands were treated as homogenous, as aggregated numbers – 'We will need so much total energy in the year X' – without the structure or without asking what kind of energy and what for. A composite of the main elements of that consensus in the United States and Great Britain can be seen in figure 1. It is a policy of strength through exhaustion in which we push very hard on all the depletable fuels we can find – coal, oil, gas and uranium – and convert them into premium energy forms (fluid fuels and especially electricity) in ever larger, more complex, more centralized plants.

Now, there are many reasons why this qualitative pattern does not work. Some are logistical; some are political; some are straightforwardly economic and become obvious if you ask 'How much capital do you have to invest in order to increase delivered energy supplies by the heat equivalent of one barrel of oil per day?' The answer is very simple: as we go from the traditional direct-fuel systems (on which our economies have been built) to offshore and Arctic and synthetic oil and gas, the capital intensity rises by a factor of about ten; and as we go from those systems in turn to central-electric systems – power stations and grids – the capital intensity goes up by another factor of ten. It is that roughly hundredfold increase in capital intensity

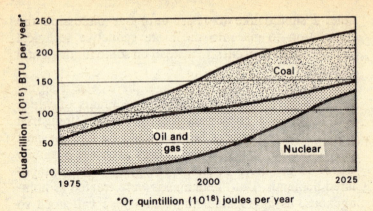

*Or quintillion (10^{18}) joules per year

Figure 1a Hard Energy Paths US

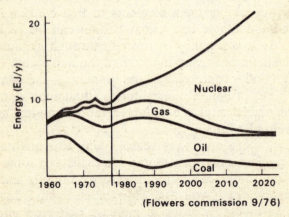

(Flowers commission 9/76)

Figure 1b Hard Energy Paths UK

that makes it impossible for any major country outside the Persian Gulf to use these high technologies, especially the electric systems, on a truly large scale, large enough to substitute for oil and gas. They are just so expensive that they are starting to look rather like future technologies whose time has passed.

Yet they are exactly the systems on which this 'hard energy path', as I shall call it, relies for most of its growth; so it is not surprising that, in a typical case, the first ten years of such a policy in the US would cost somewhat over a trillion (a million million) of today's dollars, three-quarters of it for electrification. (The number scales very similarly for Britain.) What that trillion dollars means is that the country would be putting into the energy sector not just a quarter, as now, but nearer three-quarters of all discretionary investment. If we could figure out a way to do that, we would not even have the money left to build the things that are supposed to *use* all that energy. The further up the curve we went, the heavier the burden would become.

Let me just sketch what a similar British policy might look like. This is, in fact, an official strategy in the Flowers Commission's report a couple of years ago, and although it has changed a little since, qualitatively it has not changed at all. It is still the same philosophy.

Now, these enormous investments would give us electricity coming out of our ears – indeed, we already have a massive overcapacity – but electricity substitutes only very slowly and imperfectly for oil and gas, especially in transport, so we would still in the long run be short of them: after the North Sea, what do we do for an encore? Worse than that, over half of all this enormous energy growth, as you will see later, never gets to the final users because it is lost first in conversion and then in distribution as the whole fuel chain gets less and less efficient.

Putting these £0.5–1 billion blocks of capital into things that take about ten years to build would tend to increase inflation, make utility finance unstable, and worsen unemployment because the capital is tied up, stagnant, instead of being circulated. Every big power station we build directly and indirectly loses the economy in the order of 4,000 net jobs, just by starving all other sectors of the capital that they need.

So it looks as though this approach would make our economic problems worse instead of better. And, at the same time, it would cause some serious political problems. Just to get these resources into the energy sector would require a strong central authority. In those countries (Britain not really being one of them) where there is still a semblance of a market economy in energy investment, this would be quite a change. Once we had built these big complex systems we would need equally big complex bureaucracies to run them and to say who could have how much energy and at what price.

Because these systems are centralized, they allocate the energy and the social cost or side-effects of getting it to different groups of people at opposite ends of the transmission lines, pipelines, rail-lines. It is the old story where the energy goes to New York, Los Angeles or London while the side-effects go to Wyoming, the north slope of Alaska, Appalachia, the Shetlands, the Vale of Beauvoir, Torness or any coal-town you care to name in Britain – one can multiply examples. This is an arrangement considered admirable at one end but unjust at the other, and as a result in many industrial countries there are already 'energy wars' going on – serious political conflicts (there are over sixty in the United States right now) between energy siting authorities and (for the most part) politically weak agrarian people who do not want to live in a zone of national sacrifice for the benefit of somebody at the other end of the distribution system.

These centralized systems are also vulnerable to disruption by accident or malice – especially the electric grid, which can be turned off by just a few people. If you do not like being turned off you may need stringent social controls, because this sort of vulnerability fundamentally alters the balance of power between large and small groups in our society. It is also very hard to make political decisions about technologies with compulsory, perceived hazards that are exotic, disputed, unknown, maybe unknowable; and governments faced with decisions of that kind are very tempted to substitute elitist technocracy for democratic process – 'we the experts' for 'we the people'. That is gratifying for the experts but it may lead later to a loss of legitimacy. Over all of these domestic political problems looms the larger threat of nuclear violence and coercion in a world in which, we are told, in a couple of decades from now we are likely to have some tens of thousands of bombs' worth a year of strategic materials (for example, plutonium extracted from Windscale) running around as an item of commerce in the same international community that has never been able to stop the heroin traffic.

These are some of the simple, direct, 'first-order' side-effects of this approach to the energy problem. Yet they in turn interact with each other to make new, more complex side-effects which together suggest, I think, that the cheap and abundant energy at which this policy is aimed is not really cheap at all: we are just paying for it dearly everywhere else. Maybe I should concentrate on this for a moment, because we often tend to treat energy too much in isolation. Let me, for the sake of argument, use an American model here, but I think that the British analogy is not hard to find.

Suppose Americans continue to think that energy ought to be cheap, so they continue to subsidize it with tens of billions of dollars a year of their tax money to make it look cheap. They then continue to use it wastefully and to import lots of oil, which is, of course, bad for the dollar and national independence, worse for Europe and Japan who have to compete, and disastrous for the Third World who cannot compete at all. Well, that much is generally recognized; but let us follow the argument a little further. America now has to earn the money to pay for the oil, and she has traditionally done this in three main ways. One way is to run down domestic stocks of commodities. That is inflationary; it leaves big holes in the ground; it leaves the forests looking moth-eaten. The second way is to export weapons. That is inflationary and destabilizing and immoral. Another way is to export a lot of wheat and soya beans. This puts up food prices, completely inverts the Midwestern land markets and makes the American farmers mine the soil and the ground-water (that will catch up with us). America then turns around and sells some of the wheat to the Russians who divert some of their investment from agriculture into military activities, so the Americans then have to raise their own military budget. That is inflationary, but they have to do so anyway to defend the sea lanes to bring in the oil and to defend the Israelis from all those arms they have just sold to the Arabs – an argument suggesting that the best form of Middle Eastern arms control might be American roof insulation.

Because the wheat and soya beans look important to the oil balance of trade, Americans then feel driven to develop ever more energy- and water- and capital-intensive chemical agribusiness, which destroys some of the natural life-support systems. They then feel driven to use still more fertilizers, pesticides, herbicides, irrigation, desalination, to mine Pleistocene ground-water at twenty times the recharge rate – you name it, they are doing it. Meanwhile, the soil gradually burns out, loses interest, blows or washes away – nine tons per acre per year throughout the Midwest. Who cares?

At a 10 per cent discount rate, soil in fifty years is hardly worth anything.

Meanwhile, back in the cities, because the energy looks cheap it has been substituted disproportionately for people, displacing people with black boxes. The economists call this 'increasing productivity', by which they mean *labour* productivity, and specifically they mean the labour productivity of those people who have not yet been displaced (the rest do not count). They then tell us that we need more of these energy- and capital-intensive black boxes to fuel the economic growth that they say we need to employ the people whom we have just disemployed by this very process. In any case, clearly, when we replace people with black boxes we increase poverty, inequity, alienation and crime. So we then try to spend money on things such as crime control and health care, only to find that we cannot because we have already spent the money on the energy sector, which is contributing to the unemployment and illness at which those investments were aimed.

At home, we drift gradually towards a garrison state to try to protect ourselves from some of these home-made vulnerabilities. Abroad, we strengthen oil and uranium cartels. We are not addressing rational development goals – in fact, we are competing with our trading partners to see who can export the most reactors, weapons and inflation to the Third World. This rightly encourages international distrust and domestic dissent, which entail further suspicion and repression. Meanwhile we are burning all these fossil fuels, putting carbon dioxide into the air and running the risk of destabilizing the world climate on which our marginal agriculture depends – for instance in the monsoon belt in India, and in the Midwestern bread-basket on which, decades from now, everyone is going to depend for exported food. And we are also spreading bombs all over the place.

If you ask yourself how these and similar side-effects interact with each other, what the third-order effects are and what sort of world this would be like to live in, then I think it becomes clear that you would not really want to live in it; and if, as proponents of this view claim, there is no alternative to it, then the human prospect would indeed be bleak. There would be no object to what any of us are doing. The only really useful skill to have, I suppose, would be to know how to dig a very deep hole and pull it in after you.

I think there is, however, a different way we can look at the energy problem that can lead us in a much nicer direction. I shall call it a 'soft energy path' (see figure 2).

The American version has three main technical components, which I shall take in turn: namely, using much more efficiently the energy we have; getting it increasingly from 'soft technologies' (which I shall define presently); and intelligently using fossil fuels for the transition.

The British version is due to my valued Cambridge colleague, David Oliver. Nuclear gradually disappears; gas, oil and coal are used in a transition to essentially complete reliance, around the middle of the next century or before, on soft technologies (which again I shall define in a moment). By 2025 nearly all the oil and gas are being used for feed-stocks rather than actual energy, so the saturation of soft technologies is nearly complete.

I should like to emphasize that these two evolutionary paths are distinguished not by how much energy we use nor by our choices of equipment, but primarily by their very different structural and political implica-

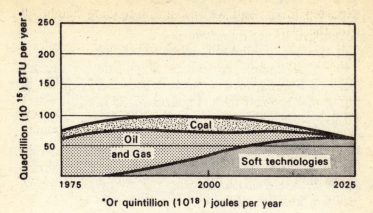

Figure 2a   Soft Energy Paths US

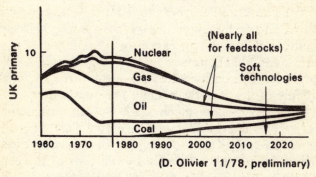

Figure 2b   Soft Energy Paths UK

tions. It is a distinction more of political economy than of mere hardware, and I shall come back to that point.

The two paths also reflect quite different views of what the energy problem is. In the hard path there is a presumption that the more energy we use the better off we are, so energy is elevated from a means to an end in itself. Whereas in the soft path, rather in the spirit of Buddhist economics, how much energy we use to accomplish our social goals is considered a measure not of our success but of our failure – just as; if you want to get to somewhere, how much traffic you have to endure to get there will not measure how well off you are but it might measure our failure to have a rational settlement pattern in which you are already near to where you want to be. The energy problem, then, that the soft path is addressing is not just where to get more energy to meet projected homogeneous demands; it starts rather at the other end of the problem. It starts by asking, 'What are our heterogeneous end-use needs (that is, what are the many different tasks we are trying to do with the energy)? And how can we do those tasks with a minimum – with, if you like, an elegant frugality – of energy *supplied in the most effective way for each task?*' This emphasis on a particular task and the best tool for it – which is the basis of all good engineering – leads, as you will see; to quite a different impression of what kinds of new energy supply make sense.

Now, let me consider the first of the three technical elements of a soft path, namely the question of 'end-use efficiency' – how much work we can wring from each unit of energy that is delivered to us. There is now ample technical evidence that in practice we can roughly double this efficiency by the turn of the century, roughly redouble it over the next quarter-century or so, and still have a way to go, entirely through 'technical fixes' – that is, measures which are now economic by normal criteria, use today's or quite often 1870's technologies, and which have no significant effect on life-styles. These include simple methods such as stuffing up the square metre of holes in your house, recovering waste heat in buildings and industry, cogenerating electricity in factories as a by-product of process steam, making electric motors and automobile engines more efficient, and so on. Now, the reason I have shown the curve of total energy needs as having a trend downwards in the long run is that as we dig into some of the slow capital stocks, such as buildings, we can actually improve the efficiency of using energy faster than the growth of what we do with it. I happen to think the classical ideas of economic growth are spherically senseless – that is, they make no sense no matter which way you look at them – but I am going to assume them anyway to save argument. I have assumed here orthodox projections of rapid growth in GNP, comfort, equity and (in the US case) population. I have assumed roughly a threefold increase in real GNP over this period. I have *not* assumed any significant changes in life-styles, settlement patterns, political organization or composition of GNP. If you happen to feel that today's values or institutions are imperfect, then you are welcome to assume some mixture of technical and social changes, which will make this all a lot easier, but I have not done that. I have carefully, and with some difficulty, kept my personal preferences separate from my analytic assumptions.

In fact, I have very much *under*estimated the purely technical scope for doing more with less energy, and to make that point I have constructed a little sociological matrix (see figure 3) showing how much energy

YEAR	BEYOND THE PALE	HERESY	CONVENTIONAL WISDOM	SUPERSTITION
1972	125 Lovins	140 Sierra Club	160 AEC	190 BuMines, FPC
1974	100 EPP (ZEG)	124 EPP (TF)	140 ERDA	160 EEI,EPRI
1976	75 Lovins	89–95 von Hippel/Lovins & & Williams/ Baudelaine For. Aff.	124 ERDA	140 EEI
1978	33 Steinhart (for 2050)	63–77 CONAES Cons. & Dem./IEA (Weinberg) Panel (for 2010)	96–101	124 Lapp
		(I) (II)	(III)	

Figure 3

41

various people thought the United States would need in the year 2000, measured in crazy units called 'quads' per year (the US now uses about 75 quads per year – about a third of all world energy use – and Britain uses about nine quads per year). I have classified these forecasts according to when they were made and according to who made them. One of the Huxleys said that all knowledge is fated to start as heresy and end as superstition, so I have those two categories with conventional wisdom included in between, and then there is the pre-heretical phase called 'beyond the pale', which means people do not even bother to read it.

Back before the embargo, people like me were saying that America could do just fine with 125 quads in the year 2000. My Berkeley colleague John Holdren was down below 100 quads – off the chart to the left. The Sierra Club was heretically suggesting 140, while the Atomic Energy Commission was secure in the conventional wisdom of 160 and the Department of the Interior and Federal Power Commission were around 190. (I think Exxon was around 230 – all pretty ambitious compared with the present 75 or so.) Then came the embargo and the Ford Foundation's Energy Policy Project, whose 100-quad scenario was not taken very seriously, but their 124-quad technical fix was, because it was lower than the Energy Research and Development Administration's 140 or the utility industry's 160 or so. Then two years ago in *Foreign Affairs Quarterly* (and in the US soft-path graph (in figure 2)) I suggested that 95 quads would be ample; but in talks I was saying 75 made much better use of the efficiency improvements we had already discovered, and some Princeton analysts, Drs von Hippel and Williams, came up with a solid 89. By then ERDA had come down from 140 to 124 – they had discovered technical fixes – and

Edison Electric Institute had come down from 160 to 140, having discovered price elasticity.

Here we are now, and an analyst in Wisconsin called John Steinhart is talking about 33 quads for the year 2050. We have just had a very distinguished National Academy of Sciences study called CONAES, whose blue-ribbon Demand Panel for the year 2010 projected 63 quads (which could have been a pure technical fix) and 77 and 96 (which were). Dr Alvin Weinberg, the grandfather of nuclear power, is now happy with 101 quads, and nuclear advocate Ralph Lapp, who believes energy and GNP march in lockstep, is now happy with 124. This matrix even has some predictive power. The US Department of Energy has just come out with its latest forecast for the year 2000 of 95 quads – with a moderately high oil price – precisely the number greeted with howls of derision when I published it in *Foreign Affairs* three years ago. That is now conventional wisdom. And the average of their low oil price cases (which I shall put over in 'superstition' because they require supernatural intervention) is 123 quads.

I should like you to observe that this is a diagonal matrix: every two years, you see, everything neatly pops down into the next column to the lower right. And we have not anywhere near hit bottom yet. We have only just discovered, for example, that if we had an energy-conscious materials policy we would nearly treble our national energy efficiency – but we did not know that, so it is not in any of these figures. You could also draw a quite similar chart for Britain, but there are fewer data points and so one cannot do it as neatly. The basic point that I want to make is that the scope for getting more work from the energy we have is truly enormous and puts quite a different complexion on how much we can do and how fast with soft technology; clearly, more can be done than we thought possible when projected energy demands were for ever soaring heavenwards.

Soft Technologies

1. There are dozens of different kinds of soft technology. Each one is used to do what it does best; none are intended as a panacea.

2. Soft technologies are renewable: they run on sun, wind, water, farm and forestry wastes, and conceivably a few other renewable flows – not on depletable fuels.

3. They are relatively simple and understandable from the user's point of view, but can still be technically very sophisticated – perhaps in the spirit of my pocket calculator. This is an extremely high-technology device. I do not quite know what goes on inside; I do not think I could make one; but what I care about as a user is that, in Fritz Schumacher's terms, this is a tool, not a machine. I run it, it does not run me. It is not some mysterious giant lurking over the horizon and presided over by some technological priesthood, but rather it is something I can make up my own mind about. I happen to like it. I sacrifice a goat to it every morning.

4./5. Soft energy technologies supply energy at the appropriate *scale* and *quality* for our range of end-use needs.

These last two kinds of appropriateness are the key arguments, so let me amplify them in turn, starting with scale.

We are often told that energy systems must be enormous to be affordable; and there are often some real economies of scale in direct construction costs. But there are also some equally real diseconomies of large scale which we simply have not counted before. For example, if you design a gas plant, power plant, refinery or whatever to be bigger and more centralized, you then need to buy a bigger, costlier distribution network to spread out all that energy to dispersed users. In the United States, this process has been brought to the point where, if you were an average residential customer for gas last year or for electricity in 1972, then you were paying about 29 cents of your utility-bill dollar actually to buy energy and the other 71 cents to get it delivered to you. That is a diseconomy of centralization.

Second, some of the energy gets lost along the way. Third, if we could mass-produce, say, power stations the way we do cars, they would cost at least ten times less than they do – but we cannot because they are too

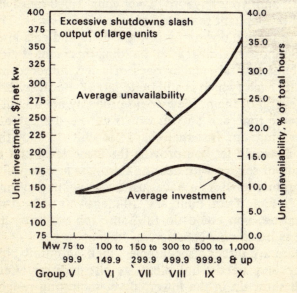

Figure 4

big. That also makes it hard to sell waste heat – to use total energy systems which would save us a lot more money. Fourth, there are some direct diseconomies of large scale which are showing up now in many international studies, particularly in Britain. Let me give a typical example – it happens to be American because it has been nicely plotted. The graph (see figure 4) shows half of all the thermal power stations commissioned in the US in a recent two-year period, and I expect that the situation would be the same in Britain. You notice that as the plants get bigger, the fraction of time they are inoperable also gets bigger: it goes up from about 10 per cent to 35 per cent, for very good technical reasons which are not going to go away. In fact, it is even worse than that, because if one of these 1,000-megawatt stations dies on you, it is embarrassing. It is rather like having an elephant die in the drawing-room, and you have to have your 1,000-megawatt stand-by elephant ready to haul the carcass away. That reserve margin ordinarily just sits there and eats interest. Suppose that instead of building this giant station, you built several smaller ones of a few hundred megawatts each (which is still quite large). Because there are several of them, they would probably not all fail at the same time and so you would not need so great a reserve margin. Just that change in unit size, for that reason, would let you provide the same level and reliability of service with about a third less new capacity. Congratulations! You have just saved about £150 million. In fact, if you built, say, 10-megawatt units at the substation, you could do the same job with about a third as much new capacity.

There are direct diseconomies, then, in unreliability and reserve needs; but there are also indirect effects which show up in the lower curve, indicating roughly how much capital we had to invest to install a given amount of new generating capacity in plants of different sizes. On classical economy-of-scale theories it should go straight up to the left, but something funny is happening because actually it is costing us *less* to install a kilowatt of capacity in a small station than in a very big one. I suspect this is because the small plant is so much *faster* to build that it reduces our exposure to interest charges, cost escalation, changes in government rules, premature completion; it gives a low-inertia, low-risk investment in a time of rapid technical and social change.

There are some other even more interesting diseconomies of scale which we have also ignored before. For example, there are all the political costs that I mentioned earlier and that rightly dominate the way we make energy decisions. (I might, by the way, single out vulnerability as a national security issue: there is no point at all in having armed forces if a few people can quietly come in and turn you off, as is now the case.) There is increased local, social and environmental stress around the sites of these big facilities. That puts quite a strain on the planning process. It is hard to find a site, so if the Central Waste Heat Generating Board finally get one, they want to pack as much capacity as possible onto it; but that makes the plant a worse neighbour than it would otherwise have been, so it is harder to get the *next* site, and the transaction costs go up exponentially. We are well into that loop. It then becomes possible to make really big mistakes (in the United States we call this the ConEd syndrome after our New York City utility).

We are encouraging oligopoly because small business cannot make big machines. What we are doing is less relevant to the needs of most of the people of the world. The personal responsibility of technologists dwindles and may even slip through the cracks as policy passes into the hands of big promotional constituencies. And anyway, as Freeman Dyson points out, big technologies are less fun to create and too big to play with, so technology may not be as innovative as it would be with smaller, simpler things that are accessible to a lot of tinkerers.

Now, I think that all of these effects are real and important; but if you like to count only what is readily countable (as I fear many people do) you will probably want to count just the first five on the list. Let me count just the first two, the costs and losses of distribution, and then do a little economics.

I was brought up as a normal healthy techno-twit, and therefore I always assumed that although soft technologies were nice they would cost more. A few years back, however, I started doing some conservative economic calculations based on real cost and performance data from real devices you can go out and buy. I shopped around carefully to get the best technology of each kind to be fair to all of them. To my astonishment, I discovered that soft technologies are in fact *cheaper* than hard technologies for the same jobs. Let us look, for example, at how much capital is required to build complete new energy systems to deliver energy to final users at a heat rate equivalent to a barrel of oil per day (see figure 5). (The British figures will differ slightly from those shown here, but the conclusions will be exactly the same.) You can see that the top part of the chart shows the steeply rising capital intensity for hard technologies. I have shown for comparison the generally much lower capital investments required to *save* a barrel per day by efficiency improvements. But let us look at the soft technologies.

Suppose you have a house. The cheapest, quickest,

ENERGY SYSTEM[A]	OP. DATE	1976 $/(BBL.DAY)[B]	FORM SUPPLIED
HARD TECHNOLOGIES			
(Traditional direct fuels	1950s-60s	2–3,000	Fuel)
Arctic & offshore oil & gas	1980s	10–25,000	Fuel
Synthetics (coal/shale)	1980s	40,000	Fuel
Central coal-EL.	1980s	170,000	EL.
Nuclear-EL. (LWR)	1980s	235,000	EL.
"TECHNICAL FIXES" TO IMPROVE END-USE EFFICIENCY			
New commercial bldgs. 1978		0–3,000	Heat/ (EL)
Common industrial & architectural leak plugging,			
better home appliances 1978		0–5,000	Heat & EL
Most heat-recovery systems 1978		5–15,000	Heat
Bottoming cycles; better motors 1978		20,000	EL.
Very thorough bldg. retrofits 1978		30,000	Heat
TRANSITIONAL FOSSIL-FUEL TECHNOLOGIES			
Coal-fired fluidized-bed gas turbine with district			
htg. & heat pumps (COP =2) 1982		30,000	Heat
Most industrial cogeneration 1979		60,000	EL. & heat
SOFT TECHNOLOGIES			
Passive solar htg.(≤100%) 1978		< 0–20,000	Heat
Retrofitted 100%-solar-neighbourhood-scale			
space & water heat 1985		20–40,000	Heat
Same, single house 1985		50–70,000	Heat
300°C solar process heat 1980		120,000	Heat
Bioconversion of farm & forestry wastes			
to alcohols/pyrolysis oil 1980		10–25,000	Fuel
Microhydroelectric plants 1980		30–140,000	EL.
Solar pond/Rankine engine 1979		120,000	EL.
Wind-EL. (Schachle/Riisager) 1979		70–185,000	EL.
Photovoltaics (Patscentre CdS) 1980		110,000	EL.

Figure 5

easiest thing to do with it is to retrofit it to the teeth – plug up the square metre of holes, insulate it, glaze it, perhaps even install heat exchangers for exhaust air and water so that you get the heat back and do not have to generate it again from scratch. Those changes are fairly expensive. They will probably cost as much as one or two thousand pounds for a leaky old detached house, but are still cheaper than not doing it. These measures are highly cost-effective even against cheap North Sea gas.

Once you have done that, in most places, including probably some parts of Britain, you will not need any heat. Your house will need less than a tenth as much heat as you need now, and that will probably be accounted for by people, windows, lights and appliances.

This could be true in most of France; Britain is a marginal case. If you still need some heat, for example if you live in the north, the cheapest method is to use passive solar heating, e.g. put a greenhouse on the south side of your house; this is being done very successfully in places such as central Norway, south-central Alaska, Montana, Wyoming – extremely severe climates, much worse than anything in Great Britain. It works at least as well as solar panels and costs a lot less. The next cheapest method is seasonal-storage active solar heating (using solar collector panels with water storage in big tanks to take you right through the winter) on a neighbourhood scale – that is, solar district heating. The next cheapest after that is to put a completely active solar system (again requiring no back-up) onto your single very efficient house. But interestingly enough, that rather fancy solar system will cost less than half as much capital as you would otherwise have to spend for a very efficient nuclear-powered electric heat pump to heat the same house. It will also cost less than the use of a synthetic-gas plant and a furnace. And so on, whether you are considering high- or low-temperature heat, portable liquid fuels for vehicles, or even electricity: although the soft technologies are *not cheap*, they are *cheaper than not having them*. They may or may not be cheaper than present oil or gas – some are and some are not – but what matters is that they are a lot cheaper than what it would cost otherwise to *replace* present oil and gas.

When I put all of these costs on the same chart, for capital cost or for a delivered energy price, I am avoiding a little find-the-lady game which the government love to play with energy costs. What they like to do is to compare with each other the costs of things they like to build, e.g. synthetic-gas plants versus various kinds of power plants. Then, when it comes to the things that they are not traditionally so excited about, such as solar heating, they like to compare those costs not with the competing hard technologies, but instead with historically cheap and heavily subsidized oil and gas, which we are running out of and which all of these things are meant to replace! So they demand of soft technologies an economic performance which hard technologies fail by a larger margin to deliver. More concretely, in the United States (and it is the same in Great Britain), for example, the Department of Energy routinely rejects as uneconomic – as costing more than a $15 barrel of oil – the more expensive kinds of solar heat and crop-and-forestry-waste alcohols because these cost as much as $25 a barrel. At the same time, the Department are proposing to give the most lavish and bizzare subsidies for things such as synthetic gas at the equivalent of $30 or $40 a barrel, or electricity at $100 a barrel. Plainly, that is bonkers (or, more formally, that leads to a misallocation). What we ought to be doing is to compare all of our investment opportunities *with each other* – not some with each other and some with the cheap oil and gas. When we do this, we find that by far the cheapest options are the efficiency improvements, then the soft and transitional technologies, then synthetic gas; and the dearest systems by far, even with heat pumps, are the central-electric systems.

This does not mean that if you decide against building some turkey like Torness you should then go out looking for another way to generate big blocks of electricity. That is not really the point. What you are interested in is how best to do the end-use jobs that would have been done with the oil and gas if you had had them in the first place. This leads me to the fifth and most important part of the definition of soft technologies: that they should supply energy of the appro-

51

priate *quality* for the tasks in question. What do we really want the energy for?

Well, to take Britain as an example, at the point where the energy is used, 66 per cent of energy needs in this country are for heat, and of that, 55 per cent is for heat below the boiling-point of water. Another 26 per cent of energy needs are for portable liquid fuels for vehicles. A total of only 8 per cent of delivered energy needs are for the premium uses that need electricity and that can give us value for money from this very special, high-quality and expensive form of energy. If you order a new power plant today, the electricity will cost the equivalent, on a heat basis, of oil at over $100 per barrel, which is seven times the world oil price, and you would be lucky to get it for that. No one would want to heat their house or water with something that costs $100 a barrel. If you were going to use it to run things that really need electricity – electronics, overhead projectors, lights, motors, household appliances, smelters, electrochemistry, arc-welders, electric railways – then you might be willing to pay that kind of price. But those premium uses, only 8 per cent of all of our delivered energy needs, are already long since filled up. We have a lot more electricity than that right now: it is more like 14 per cent or 15 per cent in the UK; with more on the way. The extra electricity that we cannot get our money's worth out of is already going where more electricity would have to go if we made still more – to be used inappropriately for low-temperature heating and cooling. Using electricity for such low-grade tasks is rather like using a forest fire to fry an egg, or cutting butter with a chainsaw. It is inelegant, expensive, messy, dangerous – and bad for chainsaws.

In other words, our energy supply problem is overwhelmingly – 92 per cent – a problem of heat and of portable liquid fuels. More electricity is simply not a rational response, because it is too slow and much too dear. Therefore, debating which kind of power station to build (which is much of what passes for energy policy these days) is completely irrelevant; it is like debating the best buy in champagne when all you need or can afford is a drink of water. And yet that irrelevancy occupies about three-quarters of our energy investment and research effort. Something is wrong here; it is a classic case of inappropriateness for the task. If, indeed, the US (to take that example) were to use its electricity efficiently in a way that is now cost-effective – I am assuming only economic rationality as conventionally defined, without any changes in life-style – the US would be just as well off with a quarter or a fifth as much total electricity. The present hydro-electric capacity, small-scale hydro, and a bit of wind could cover that, but no thermal power plants of any kind would be needed. That little thought-experiment shows how far out of step we are with the economically efficient ideal of supplying energy only of the quality needed for the task in hand.

If we were to do that, we would largely eliminate the costs and losses of further converting the energy; and if we were to supply it at the right scale for each task, we would largely eliminate the costs and losses of distributing it, because it would already be where we wanted it. Those two kinds of losses – conversion and distribution – dominate growth in a hard energy path: that is, they make the primary fuels that we pour into the hopper run away from the delivered end-use energy that actually gets to us. All the space in between, making up nearly all the growth, represents losses. Whereas in the soft path, by supplying energy in the right way for each task, we would largely squeeze out those losses.

We would literally be doing more with less.

Recently, and especially in the past year or two, we have seen extraordinarily rapid technical progress – mainly outside the official programmes – in the development of a wide range of soft technologies. In an article in *Annual Review of Energy* (pp 477–517 [1978]), I have shown that the soft technologies now in or entering commercial service around the world, and suited to British conditions, are already more than enough to meet virtually all of our end-use needs. When I say that there are enough soft technologies already, I am excluding things that are not here yet, such as cheap solar cells; but I am including the best present art, if you shop around carefully, in passive and active solar heating, solar process heat for industry, converting farm and forestry residues into liquid fuels to run efficient vehicles (there is, apparently, enough to run the British transport sector), hydro power and wind – in some cases for electricity, in others for heat-pumping, water-pumping or compressing air to run machines. If you add up the best present art in each of those categories and use each one to do what it does best, it becomes apparent that they are more than enough. We shall have even better ones, but we have enough to be getting on with.

And yet even though we have these soft technologies, it will still take a long time to get them all in place. It might take of the order of fifty years, because historically, the energy system being so big and sluggish, it has taken about that long to do anything. So we will certainly need, meanwhile, to buy that time by briefly and sparingly using fossil fuels for a transition, in clean ways that we can plug the soft technologies into as they become available. There is a nice example in Enköping, Sweden, where there is a commercial district-heating plant containing a fluidized-bed boiler, which will surpass the strictest air quality standards burning high-sulphur coal with no scrubber. It will also burn any kind of oil, gas, wood, peat, trash or energy studies (that is my favourite). And the district-heating grid of insulated hot-water pipes around town is so designed that it can later be readily converted to seasonal-storage solar district-heating, which costs only half as much as heating one building at a time – in fact, it competes nicely with $8-a-barrel oil right now. It is a very good deal.

I think that with such methods and with really quite a modest and orderly coal-mining programme, gradually phasing out over several generations of coal-miners, we can squeeze down the oil-and-gas wedge from both sides, stretch out the North Sea, get off our long-term import hook and leave some of the frontier oil and gas in the ground where they cannot get into mischief. We would be doing all this not by wiping the slate clean, but by starting where we are, doing things differently from now on and retiring inappropriate stocks through normal attrition. We would not be abolishing big technologies, but rather saying that they have an important place which they have already filled up. We can take advantage of the big systems we have (like the National Grid) without multiplying them further – that is what the argument is about. It is in no sense an anti-technology programme. It involves some exciting technical challenges, but of a different and to some people an unfamiliar kind: making things sophisticated in their simplicity, not in their complexity. I cannot resist a quick example of what I mean by that. Some aerospace engineers in the United States put up an extremely expensive and unsuccessful wind machine in Ohio. They spent something of the order of £10,000 on a computerized system of electronic instruments to shut down this wind machine if it started vibrating too much, so that it would not shake itself to pieces. The Danish engineers who built the old Gedser mill some decades ago solved the same problem in a much simpler way. In the tower of their wind machine they had a shallow saucer with a big steel ball in it, and if the whole thing started to shake too much, this ball would eventually slop out of the saucer and fall down, with a string attached to it pulling a switch. That is a much higher order of engineering.

My reason for setting up these two paths, you may recall, was as a vehicle for ideas, so let me draw a few comparisons between them. I have suggested already that the soft path has a lower capital cost; it has a better cash flow because things are quicker to build and to pay back, so more can be done with a given amount of working capital; and except for the biomass systems, soft path projects do not use any fuel, so the final advantage in delivered energy price (which is what the consumer cares about) is large, typically a factor of three or so. Further, a soft path is not only cheaper, but is also faster than the hard path: that is, per pound invested, it gives you more energy and money and jobs back more quickly. There are three main reasons for this: one is that projects in a soft path have construction times of days, weeks or months, not ten years; second, they sell into a vastly larger market, tens of millions of households, not a handful of utilities; and third, the soft-technology wedge is made up of dozens of components, each held back by different problems largely independent of the others. Small-scale hydro has regulatory problems, passive solar heating is held back by the need to retrain architects and builders, but these and others like them are independent problems. You can, therefore, envisage dozens of slowly growing individual wedges independently adding up by sheer strength of numbers to very rapid total growth. It is not at all the same as having a few monolithic technologies held back by the same problems everywhere at once.

For the same reason, the risk of technical failure is much lower when spread among dozens of fairly simple things known to work, than if you put all your eggs in a few baskets such as synthetic-gas plants and breeder reactors which may or may not work. The soft path is environmentally much more benign and it hedges our bets on the important climatic problems (such as carbon dioxide) by getting us out of the whole fossil-fuel-burning business as quickly as possible.

The soft path is suited not only to urban and industrial societies, but also to modern development concepts. Let us take as an example two ways to make nitrogen fertilizer in India. One way is to build a single Western-style fertilizer plant. Another way is to build roughly 26,000 village-scale gobar gas plants. These turn out to have a lower total capital cost (about half that much with Chinese technology); they have zero foreign exchange drain, and provide over a hundred times more jobs in a country with a labour surplus and a capital shortage. Instead of being a net energy consumer, they are such a copious producer of methane that they can meet virtually all of the cooking, lighting and pumping needs of the village – and that is half of all the energy needs in India at present. What is happening now, of course, is that the cow dung is burned as cooking fuel in open fires, and all the nitrogen and most of the heat goes up in smoke, which blinds people. Whereas with a biogas plant you have a better fertilizer and this clean and efficient fuel. You break the cycle of firewood shortage, deforestation and erosion. Clearly, in an Indian context, this is an example of a very powerful development tool – which is why China has installed about five million biogas plants in the past six years.

Another important geopolitical side-effect of the soft path is that it gives the main nuclear countries the political leverage to promote a world psychological climate of denuclearization in which it comes to be viewed as a mark of national immaturity to have or to want reactors or bombs. What offers this leverage, I think, is that the nuclear business is rapidly turning into a pumpkin. This remarkable graph (see figure 6) shows the range of official projections for how much nuclear capacity the US was to have installed in the year 2000 as a function of when the government made the projection. You can see from linear extrapolation that it should hit zero around the end of this year. It will actually come to rest somewhere between zero (if the plants are phased out) and around 120 gigawatts if they are not. That is, if the net reactor ordering rate (which in the United States has been getting more and more *negative* in the past four years) was miraculously to come *up* to zero, so that everything in the pipeline came dribbling out, then in the year 2000, US nuclear power (which is roughly half the world total) would be down in the firewood league, supplying rather less than 3 per cent of present total delivered energy use.

Well, that could be called a local political eccentricity; we all know about the American regulatory problems. So I have tried the same graph for Canada, which has had none of these regulatory problems – the government just builds reactors wherever it wants them. The graph for Canada is so identical that you could put it right on top of the US graph and not tell them apart. This indicates to me a *market* effect, that this is a technology suffering from an incurable attack of market forces. (Fans of Adam Smith might say, 'The Invisible Fist strikes again!') Indeed, if you draw the

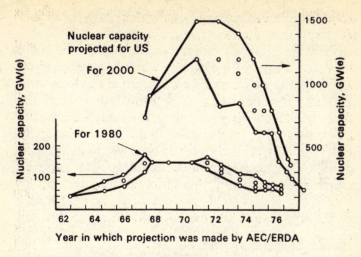

Figure 6

same graph for Britain, France, Germany, Japan, any nuclear country of note, you get essentially the same graph, for the same basic economic reason. This means that nuclear power will not amount to much before the oil runs out unless, among other things, there is a simply enormous and sustained bail-out with public money to keep the industry alive. I do not see any prospect of that, even in Great Britain, because it is simply too expensive.

Given this political background, suppose countries such as Britain and the United States do three things. First of all, suppose we say that however much we love nuclear power, we love the market even more and will accept its verdict. We will not bail out this technology; we will design an orderly terminal phase for this unfortunate aberration and will try to make the market, such as it is, more efficient – so that nuclear resources continue to be rapidly recycled into the tasks of a soft energy path because it makes more sense. Second, that we will freely and unconditionally help any other country that wants to follow our example – an example for which many are now waiting. Third, that we will try to link those efforts with whatever we can do on the much slower and more difficult task of mutual strategic arms reduction, treating them as interrelated parts of the same problem with intertwined solutions – so we do not go on saying, for example, that it is patriotic for us to have bombs but irresponsible for India to have them. Now, nobody can guarantee that this three-pronged approach to stopping proliferation of nuclear weapons would be fully successful. But there is a growing feeling in the arms control community that it is much more likely to work than anything else we have thought of, and that accepting and building constructively upon the collapse of the nuclear enterprise in all countries where it has to face any kind of market test (and even in those, such as Britain, where it does not) is a prerequisite for any effective nonproliferation policy.*

The last comparison I want to make between these two paths, and the one that really defines the difference between them, is political. Each of these two paths entails difficult political problems of very different kinds: in the hard path, mainly such problems as centrism, vulnerability, technocracy, inequity, autarchy; in the soft path, such problems as pluralism – getting used to the idea of doing with a hundred million choices what we would otherwise have done with a few big projects run from Whitehall, getting used to the idea that, in a country this big and this diverse, with a problem as fine-grained as energy central management may be more a part of the problem than a part of the

* This thesis is expanded in the July 1980 *Foreign Affairs Quarterly*.

solution. For some central managers, that may be a traumatic adjustment. But no energy future is going to be free of social problems. What we have to choose are the kinds of problems we prefer. There is no free lunch – some lunches are just cheaper than others. And it seems to me that the social problems of the soft path are a lot more tractable, and get easier as they go on. In fact, the social and economic advantages are so great that, if we let them show themselves, a soft path would largely implement itself through existing market and political processes.

To make this a reality, we need to do three main things. First of all, at a county and local level, we need to clear away a long, messy list of institutional barriers, or what an economist would call market imperfections, that impede efficiency and soft technologies: obsolete building codes and lending regulations, architectural fee structures that encourage inefficiency, restrictive utility practices, inequitable access to capital, split incentives between builders and buyers or landlords and tenants (why should landlords stuff up the cracks round the windows if you pay the heating bill?), and lack of good information on what is available. These are all difficult problems, but if we are not clever enough to solve them, I certainly do not think we shall be clever enough to solve the more formidable institutional problems that are already bringing the hard path grinding to a halt. Second, we ought to stop spending a great deal of money – nobody knows how much it is in Britain, but in the United States it is about $100 billion a year in tax and pricing subsidies – trying to deceive ourselves into thinking that conventional fuel and power are much cheaper than they really are. In California this has reached the point where the state is giving a 55 per cent tax credit to people who use solar energy, yet that subsidy cannot compete with the larger Federal one being given to Alaskan gas. So we start with solar heat which is cheaper than gas, subsidize them both at great expense, and finish with the gas looking cheaper. Third, we ought to move gradually and fairly, as I think we know how, towards charging ourselves for depletable fuels – indeed, for depletable resources – what it will cost us to replace them in the long run. Not doing that is just a sophisticated way of stealing from our children.

It will not be easy to do any of those three things, but I think it will be easier than not doing them. If it is handled right, a soft path can have great political appeal, because unlike a hard path it offers simultaneous advantages for almost every constituency – which is rather good news for politicians. It offers, for example, jobs for the unemployed, capital for the CBI (otherwise the capital goes mostly to energy and is never seen again), savings for consumers, chances for small business to innovate and for big business to recycle itself, environmental protection for conservationists, better national security for the military, exciting technologies for the secular, a rebirth of spiritual values for the religious, world order and equity for globalists, energy independence for isolationists, radical reforms for the young, traditional virtues for the old, civil rights for liberals, local autonomy for conservatives. Admittedly, it does not coincide with the perceived short-term interests of a few powerful institutions which I think have not yet grasped its opportunities and hence wrongly see it as a threat. But it does run with, not across, our political grain.

It also cuts through the kinds of ideological disputes that are now stalling energy policy. Take as an example the recent antics in the US Senate, where it was said that before the US could even start on a national energy policy, agreement had to be reached about things

such as price versus regulation, capitalism versus socialism, Hamilton versus Jefferson, the role of the oil
companies, the future shape of the society. Americans
have never agreed about any of those things and never
shall, but if they are made a prerequisite to an energy
policy hell will freeze over first (maybe literally).
Whereas in a soft path, those kinds of disagreement
become pretty irrelevant. If you are an economic traditionalist and care about what is cheapest for you, then
you build your solar collector because it is cheaper than
not building it. If you are a worker, you might build it
because it gives you far more and better jobs than
building power stations. If you are an environmentalist,
you might build it because it is benign; if you are a
social transformationalist, you might build it because
it is autonomous. But the point is, it is still the same
collector. You do not have to agree, before or after,
about why you built it. It is motive-free. We have an
overwhelming consensus that energy husbandry and
soft technologies are desirable, that they are a good
path to follow. We have no consensus, and I doubt we
ever shall, on anything else in energy policy. So perhaps what we ought to be doing is adding up the bits
that we agree about because they are enough, and then
we can forget the bits we do not agree about because
they will be superfluous. We have never tried before
to design an energy policy around consensus, but it
seems time we started.

And yet the time remaining is short, because although each of the paths embraces infinite variations
on a theme, there is a sense in which they are mutually
exclusive. I do not mean, as some people have supposed, that hard and soft *technologies* are *technically
incompatible*, because they are not. There is nothing
to stop you, technically, from putting solar panels on
top of Dungeness B – it might help it to work better.

Indeed, in a soft energy path you would start with a bunch of hard technologies and end up with a bunch of soft ones fifty or seventy-five years later; in between, they would coexist as their mix gradually shifted, as you retired one and brought in the other. But that shift takes place within a social and political context which gives rise to three kinds of 'exclusivity. The first is cultural: simply put, each one of these worlds makes the other kind of world harder to imagine. Where we are now is an excellent example: a lot of people cannot imagine any approach to the energy problem other than what they have been doing for the past thirty years – just because of cultural conditioning. Second, each of these paths builds up thick layers of organization, laws, habits, policy actions which inhibits the other – just as, today, a host of institutional barriers left over from the cheap oil era are locking us into more of the same, not something different. Third, these paths compete for resources. Every pound, every tonne of oil, every bit of work and skill and political attention, and (most precious) every year that we devote to those very demanding hard technologies is a resource we cannot also use to do the tasks of a soft path urgently enough so that they cohere – because the timing matters. In this sense projects such as Torness and synthetic gas are not only unnecessary; they are positive encumbrances whose resource commitments threaten to push the soft-technology wedge so far off into the future that before we can get to it, our fossil-fuel bridge to it will literally have been burnt.

So we ought, with due deliberate speed, to be choosing one or the other of these broad patterns before one has foreclosed the other, or before proliferation has foreclosed both. We ought to be asking where we could get to in fifty years and then work back to see how to get there smoothly (as some of my colleagues are now doing), rather than continue by incremental ad-hocra-cy, one power station at a time. We ought to be using those relatively cheap fuels and the cheap money made from them, thriftily, to capitalize a transition as direct as possible straight to our ultimate energy-income tech-nologies; because once cheap money and cheap fuel are gone, we shall not have another chance to get there.

At the heart of these issues is a difference in per-spective about our species and its works. Some people who are impressed and fascinated by the glittering achievements of technology say that if we would only have faith in human ingenuity (theirs) we shall see the second coming of Prometheus, bringing us undreamed-of freedom and plenty. Some other people say that we ought to plan for something rather more modest, lest we find instead undreamed-of tyrannies and perils, and that even if we had a clean and unlimited energy source we would lack the discipline to use it wisely, for we have not even learned yet to cope properly with the first coming of Prometheus. Such people are really saying, first, that energy is not enough to solve the ancient problems of the human spirit; and second, that those technologists who claim 'no acts of God can be permitted' (Hannes Alfvén) are guilty of *hubris*, the human sin of divine arrogance. Energy policy offers us today an opportunity, perhaps our last, to foster in our society a greater humility: one that springs from an appreciation of the essential frailty of the human design.

Discussion

How are we going to adopt a soft, feminine, Mother Earth technology, when we lose our machismo?

Margaret Mead has criticized the terms 'hard' and 'soft' for precisely this reason – that they arouse anxieties in the middle-aged men that run the world. I think the problem is perhaps not quite as severe as you might expect.

I speak to many high-technology groups around the world, and what I often do is describe for them a number of simple, elegantly effective devices such as a solar pond or a passive solar greenhouse, and then ask for a show of hands on who is impressed and excited by these devices. A few years ago I would get half, now I get about three-quarters, right in the centres of the highest technologies there are. I've even met a great many solar engineers in the past year who until recently were nuclear engineers, but they've decided that that isn't where their career future lies.

However, I am more concerned, just as you are, about recycling those technologists for whom something doesn't have technical sex appeal unless it's big, electric, made of exotic materials, computer-designed and has brass knobs all over it. We have a really striking example of this educated incapacity in Boston: Boeing Vertol, the aerospace people, were making Underground carriages. Their first design for a door had 1,300 parts, With some difficulty they sweated it down to about three hundred. Maybe the doors might work now, but the engineers had become so sophisticated that they couldn't design a door any more.

I think that in a genuinely soft and non-violent context, high technologists can get excited. But they need a little stirring up, and that's a very important task for the engineering educators.

Does a soft energy path include lower economic growth?

That would be highly consistent with it, but the analysis that my colleagues and I have done, and all the graphs you saw, assume a faster classical economic growth than does the government. I do not think it makes any sense, but I have assumed it to show that you could do it with a soft energy path. It would come unstuck for a lot of reasons, it would be a daft thing to do, but you could do it if you wanted to and energy would not be the constraint. I think it's important, therefore, to discredit the idea that we shall freeze in the dark if we don't use a lot more energy.

Let me leave you with a little story of how this was turned around in Franklin County, Massachusetts, which may seem a long way from Britain, but perhaps it's not that far. It's the poorest county in Massachusetts, a wooded area with some old decaying mill-towns and a lot of rather tenuous farms. About fifty citizens in the county have spent the past year looking at their energy future. They held a meeting a couple of months ago to see how they'd got on. It was a folksy New England-style town meeting. First of all, they agreed that the average household in the county was sending nearly £700 out of the county every year to pay for energy. That drain on the county economy – you might think of it as a bucket with a hole in it, since most of the money goes straight to Venezuela and they never see it again – that drain was £12 million a year, which equals the combined pay-roll of the county's ten biggest employers.

If they were lucky enough to achieve the *lowest* official forecast of energy demand growth and energy price increase to the year 2000, then in that year the average household would be sending out of the county not £700 but nearly £2,700 (constant £) just to pay for energy. To keep that sort of a leaky bucket topped up, the biggest single employer in the county today would have to clone itself every year from now to 2000! And at this point the Chamber of Commerce people in the audience turned white and said, 'That's absolutely impossible; we can't do that.' They'd never seen it worked out before. Then the group went through the conservation figures, such as how to stop living in a sieve, and the soft path supply figures – how they could do passive and active solar retrofits for heating, run their vehicles on alcohol from the sustained yield of part of the unallocated public woodlots, cover their electricity if a local engineering firm put up wind machines on a two-mile ridge section of a present transmission-line right of way, or how they could do it six times over with their microhydro within the county. I forget whether this would cost a little more or a little less than £12 million a year, but it doesn't much matter, because you've just plugged up the leaky bucket. All the money is now staying in the community, in the county; you have the local jobs and the local multiplier.

At this point in the meeting, it was the utility and Chamber of Commerce people who were out there leading the rest of the group, saying, 'This is obviously what we have to do, because it's the only thing that makes sense. So let's get on with it! What do we do first?' Ever since that meeting the whole county has been buzzing like an inverted beehive, figuring out how to construct their own soft energy path, because for them, as for the several hundred other communities around North America that have already been through this process, the energy problem for the first time was reduced to a sufficiently fine-grained and concrete level that people could see it as *their problem*. They could address it with their own resources in ways with which they were intimately familiar. Once people see the energy problem in that way, they simply go out and solve it, just as they've always solved problems.

III

Vernacular Values

Ivan Illich

Fritz Schumacher intuitively appealed to aesthetics as a fundamental category that is necessary for any sound determination of values in use, as a necessary category which does not allow operational verification in the ordinary sense, and which is independent of other categories that economists usually use. In his writings, if I have interpreted them correctly, beauty means that particular appreciation of work and of works, of process and output, that is characteristic for each culture and that at the same time rigorously eschews cross-cultural measurement as a margin of preference.

I would like to say something about the way we look at values, and how economic measurement as well as beauty or goodness can be referred to them. I want to invite you to follow me to Spain in the year 1492. Now 1492 is a very important date in Spain: the Jews, among them my ancestors, were expelled from Toledo, and the last Moors had to give up Granada and the fortress of the Alhambra. In the spring of that year Christopher Columbus had left with his three ships for the Indies and discovered America, without any report of it yet having come to Europe. In that year in the fall, Don Elio Antonio de Nebrija published what turns out in retrospect to be the very first grammar of any modern European language (there were old grammars of Latin and Greek, but no modern European grammar). He presented a draft of this grammar to Queen Isabella la

Catolica, an extraordinary woman who led her armies in golden armour and then in the evening gathered around her in her tent the humanists of early Renaissance Europe, who treated her as an equal.

Nebrija dedicated to her the first edition of the grammar, published in 1492, and in the Introduction he defended his undertaking in answer to an objection raised by the Queen. A few months ago, I had an opportunity to translate the Introduction to this grammar, which is not available in English. I see in it the best description of the birth of the industrial age, and I want to read it to you:

> My illustrious Queen, whenever I ponder over the tokens of the past that writing has preserved for us I return for ever to the same conclusion: language has for ever been the mate of empire and always shall remain its comrade. Together language and empire start, together they grow and flower, and together they decline.

Please notice how language is treated as a feminine mate, please notice the betrothal of *armas y lettras*, military and university, right there in 1492. Please notice how the ever-changing patterns of vernacular speech may now be held up against the standard of language that measures them, that measures their improvement and debasement. Quote again:

> Castilian went through its infancy at the time of the Judges, it waxed in strength under Alphonse the Wise who gathered laws and histories and who had many Arabic and Latin works translated.

Notice that Alphonse was the first European monarch who used his native language as his tool to insist that he was no more a Latin king. Notice that his translators were mostly Jews who did not like to trans-

71

late into the Church's Latin, and who used instead what they believed to be the vernacular tongue in order to write their translations. Notice Nebrija's awareness that the standard language can be strengthened when it is used for the writing of history, as a medium for translation and as an embodiment of law. He goes on:

> This our language followed our soldiers who went abroad to rule; it spread to Aragon, to Navara, and hence to Italy, wherever, my lady, you sent your armies. The scattered bits and pieces of Spain [it is one of the first places where the term 'Spain' appears instead of 'Castilia'] were thus gathered and joined into one single Kingdom.

Notice the role of the soldier, who forges new worlds and creates a new role for the cleric, the pastor and educator, who has to teach the language. He continues:

> So far this Castilian language has been left by us loose and unruly, and in just a few centuries this language has changed beyond recognition because comparing what we speak today with the language of five hundred years ago, we notice a difference and diversity that could not be greater if these were two alien tongues.

Notice how in this sentence language and life are torn asunder, how the language of Castilia is treated as if, like Latin and Greek, it was already dead. Instead of the constantly evolving vernacular, Nebrija is referring to something totally different, a timeless colloquial, that must be produced like a commodity and taught to people. He clearly reflects the split that at this moment comes into the Western perception of values – here the 'vernacular', there 'taught mother tongue'. Although I find a transitory use of the term 'mother tongue' in the eleventh century, when certain German ic monks tried to defend themselves against an invasion from France and called the language they taught 'mother tongue', the term does not appear until this period. 'Taught mother tongue' here is a new commodity which people need; 'vernacular' there is something which is loose and unruly. Nebrija again:

> To avoid these very variegated changes I have decided to turn the Castilian language from a loose possession of the people into an artifact so that whatever shall henceforth be said or written in this language, shall be of standard coinage, of a coinage that can outlast the times.

I find here the theory of industrial production, the theory of progress, development, enrichment in the service sector expressed four hundred years before so-called economists were willing to apply it to the goods sector. 'Development', 'progress', what do they mean but substitution of a commodity produced under bureaucratic supervision for a vernacular activity which today, because we consider it secondary, we usually call a subsistence activity, and which people until now have been able to generate for themselves? He goes on:

> Greek and Latin have been governed by art and thus have kept their uniformity throughout two thousand years. Unless the like be done for our language, in vain your majesty's chroniclers shall praise your deeds, your labour will not outlast more than a few years, and we shall continue to feed on Castilian translations of foreign tales about our kings. Either your feats will fade with changes in the language or they will roam among aliens abroad, homeless, without a dwelling in which they can settle for ever.

Please notice how Nebrija proposes to substitute for the vernacular speech of the people a device, an *arti-*

ficio, as he says in Spanish. 'Unrulish speech shall henceforth be substituted by standard coinage.'

We may also say that it would be so much simpler to standardize electrical production and use. I just want to point out to you that I think we cannot really get to the bottom of the ambiguities unless we become aware that the commodity intensity of our world perception, as Leiss in his brilliant little book *The Limits to Satisfaction* calls it, has roots which go back much further than what is usually called 'the Industrial Age'.

Nebrija has a new perspective on power and rule. He wants to teach people the language of clerks, to tighten their speech and to subject their utterances to the rule of the clerk, because for Queen Isabella language was perceived as a domain. Before he wrote this defence of his undertaking, she had sent back to him the draft which he had presented to her in the spring of 1492. She said to him:

> It is impressive that finally somebody has done for our Castilian tongue what so far has been done only for the sacred tongues of antiquity. But I am aghast at the uselessness of this undertaking which has taken Nebrija so many years, because a grammar is a tool to teach language and I do not see why spoken language should be taught.

She goes on with a glorious royal statement on linguistics:

> Because in our kingdoms every single subject is made by nature in such way that growing up he obtains a perfect dominion over his tongue and it does not behove the king to interfere in this domain.

Nebrija argued with the Queen in order to tell her that a new age had arrived in which language ceases to be a domain, but becomes instead a product to be delivered to people.

I would call for language accounting. Energy accounting was something a few of us began to talk about, ten years ago; today it is quite acceptable. We know how much energy is in each pound of meat that we buy at our neighbourhood store. We are just now at the point where the cost of teaching mother tongue in rich and poor countries is more or less the same as the cost of fuel production. The energy crisis is for me an interesting point, because it is the point at which the curve of fuel costs takes off more steeply than the cost of education. We have reached the point at which language accounting becomes a necessity because huge amounts of money are spent on teaching people their mother tongue.

Something has changed fundamentally in our attitude to language. According to a study in Toronto made some fifty years ago, it was estimated that one out of ten words which a man has heard when he reaches the age of twenty are words which were spoken to him as a member of a crowd, in church, in the military, or in school. Nine out of ten words were either spoken to him or overheard by him while somebody whom he could touch and feel and smell was saying them to somebody else. Today, the proportion has been reversed. About nine out of ten words which we hear are spoken either to a crowd or, much more generally, through a loudspeaker. I am concerned with discussing the structural difference between a colloquial tongue which is the result of my absorbing what people really say to each other with meaning, and a language which people get from actors, who with great phoney conviction declaim what speech-writers have written for them. What fascinates me in the field of linguistics is that this kind of analysis is almost non-existent.

Shortly after I had discovered Nebrija's Introduction to his grammar, I was invited to New York by a former pupil of mine, now a social worker and married, who was living voluntarily in a very miserable slum in the East Bronx with his family. He wanted me there to co-sign a petition for pre-kindergarten language instruction for the underprivileged children who lived in the area. This is an area of the South Bronx where well over half of all the houses have been burned down during the last three summers, partly by the people who live in them who want to destroy their apartments so that they can get access to better public housing, partly by the landlords who cannot pay the taxes, partly by the Mafia, partly by the gang wars. We went into one of the few buildings that was still standing: one of those vertical slums built in the early Kennedy years. By the way, that particular building has been closed down in the meantime by the police. Because of its purely physical characteristics they do not consider it to be defendable, with the rate of murder being so high. Anyone who knows New York knows these situations.

We went from apartment to apartment. To Jamaican, to Puerto Rican, to Southern White, to Southern Black homes, where I saw children who even at ten could not speak a word, although the television was blaring, sometimes two televisions in the same welfare apartment. After I had seen that, I refused completely to sign the petition. I said, 'This is only a means of pretending that people who live in uninhabitable houses can find a home in their language.' He did not understand me. The conversation was desperate. He had invited me to dinner, and I went very much afraid that the meal would end badly. I met his wife and his three children, the oldest of whom is six, and then at dinner I observed that these two people, generous people beyond any question, who live in an area from which everyone else flees because it is too dangerous and violent, *did not speak to their children.* Rather, at every moment they acted as if *in loco magistri*, not the teacher in place of the parent but the parent deputed by the teacher. They taught their three young children English either by speaking to them as if they were in the classroom, or by saying things to me so simply and so clearly (although it was not at all what we wanted to discuss) that the children also could understand them. There, I understood how commodity intensity, dependence on products, could be rooted right in the family, how vernacular language could be destroyed.

Fritz Schumacher propagated 'intermediate technology'. With the greatest respect and in honour of Fritz, I wonder how he would have reacted if I had said to him: 'One way to say most radically what you wanted to say all your life would be to speak about "vernacular technology".' Vernacular is an old Latin word used for technical purposes in Roman law. Vernacular means, above all, a slave born in my home to a slave woman whom I own. It is a slave picked up from the womb and not from the market. It means the donkey who is born from my own she-donkey. Vernacular also means the food that I gather or the wood that I take from common land, as opposed to the wood that is a commodity, that I have to buy. It is the technical term in Latin for the inverse of commodity, for the inverse of that which must be derived in one way or another from exchange values. It was Varo, the great Roman grammarian, who used the word for the first time in order to designate those words which are grown in our own garden, as opposed to *peregrina*, pilgrims who have settled in the home. He made the distinction between the word derived from the outside by some kind of teaching, and the word grown among us. One thousand years or more after Varo, the Codex of Theodosius still uses the term *vernaculum* for something that a man values and has the right to defend by law, something that he has not derived from the market.

The last thirty years have given us four or five major attempts to designate analogues for goods and services which are not generated within the economic system. We oppose social production to economic production; with Polanyi we oppose pre-market traders to traders of commodities. We speak about use values which are pure, in contrast to exchange values which sometimes also have use value for the ultimate receiver – and consumer – of them. For each one of these highly technical terms to designate that which we do without being paid for it and without intent to exchange it, that which we and others around us value without ever having destined it for the market – for these values we have words such as use value, home economy, domestic economy, and in the Polanyi tradition, non-marketable trading. But each of these terms first is technical, and second is by now loaded down with ideological connotations. I wonder if it would be possible, in the tradition of Schumacher, to launch the term 'vernacular value' for these things which individuals or primary groups do or make without destining them for the market. Here is a Gandhian difficulty. Gandhi spoke about *khadi* (homespun cloth) as a commodity and caused unspeakable confusion in modern India. Now *khadi* is being sold as a village-produced commodity, which is exactly the opposite of the vernacular.

If we may speak about vernacular values as the opposite of commodities, in the broadest sense, commodities which receive their value from market forces or from economic planning, then we can also introduce a distinction in technologies. We can distinguish between technology which is primarily at the service of increasing the commodity intensity of a society (that is, the possibility of defining the needs of ever larger groups of population in terms of the goods or services which are being generated for them), as opposed to technology in the service of vernacular use. I do not want to use the term 'production', or 'vernacular' production, because in American English production refers entirely to the generation of commodities. If this were possible then we could say that the most radical inversion in the orientation of technical improvements, if they were analysed or evaluated, would be the degree to which they increased the vernacular domain in a society. This does not mean that we shall cease to improve, render softer and more efficient the production of commodities, but that we shall move towards a society which places at the centre of its political, legal and ethical concerns the increase of the vernacular domain, and considers commodities as desirable primarily when represented as tools through which that domain can be further expanded. At present our political, social, psychological and technical concern is to produce more and more commodities in order to arrive at an ever more equitable distribution of them. In an inverse society that places, not the economic sector, but the vernacular sector of use-value generation at the centre of its concerns, precisely the opposite would be the case.

Discussion

Which is vernacular, Having or Being?

Let me tell you a story: I sing horribly badly. I never dare to sing when I'm with others, but I like to hum when I'm alone. I was walking down the street in Nice recently, humming, when I noticed a man who was walking towards me. When he got to within about five yards of me, he suddenly turned away and started to cross the road. But then, seeming to recognise me he came over and said, 'Aren't you so and so?' I said, 'Yes, why did you move away?' 'Well,' he replied, 'I heard you singing so I thought you were either drunk or mad and I didn't recognize you.' In the village where I live near Cuernavaca there were four bands twelve years ago, each with about ten instruments (the population of the village is no more than 1,200). Then the loudspeaker came in. Last year, for the first time, the village invited for the feast day a group of musicologists from the university to sing to our village the songs which four different orchestras were able to sing twelve years ago.

When Queen Isabella said, 'Each man is born to have a perfect dominion of his tongue,' she spoke about that small beauty which a language is, a domain on which a certain kind of power cannot trespass. In societies where language is used that way, it is well known that not only do the majority of people know

80

sayings and riddles and some bits of old stories by heart, carefully transmitted without change from generation to generation, but that creative poetry is also widely spread. Somebody spoke to me, as I came in here, about Malaysia: 'I have seen people, the poorest people, on the street corners, sitting there all night composing *fantungs*.' You make a verse of two lines, then I do the the same; we might go on through a whole moon-night. Quite obviously, this is not possible in a society in which taught mother tongue has changed environmental conditions so that the vernacular cannot be lived any more, because the scale in intercourse which makes the vernacular possible no longer exists. When even one vehicle in a society moves faster than 25 k.p.h. and is publicly financed, or its infrastructure is publicly financed, then what Dufis calls 'generalized velocity' inevitably declines and very quickly the domain for vernacular movement is destroyed. You can't even pick up a newspaper without jumping into a car.

The challenge here is to locate the point at which the production of a commodity, be it goods or services, be it energy or mother tongue, reaches that threshold beyond which it interferes with physical energy and with vernacular language. In other words the point at which commodity production in any single major area has the ultimate environmental impact of taking out of the environment precisely those conditions which make possible the generation of vernacular values in that area. When does the acceleration of traffic render total locomotion less effective and less enjoyable? I think that this happens precisely when it interferes with the environmental conditions for the vernacular domain.

Ivan Illich

How does one escape from the global classroom?

By the practice of the politics of self-fulfilling prophecy. When I say that this is the moment for the policy of self-fulfilling prophecy, I am suggesting that this is the moment for the rise of techno-fascism which administers soft technology, which imposes, almost, the choice of soft technology as the only form in which we can keep society viable at every higher levels of commodity dependence. On the other hand, it is the moment for a modernized balance between the vernacular and the industrial market of a commodity domain.

What do I mean by self-fulfilling prophecy? What Amory Lovins so brilliantly, intelligently and with great facility told us, something which none of us, if we are responsible, can excuse ourselves for not having known before. People who come to the Schumacher Lectures should know all this. But by putting it correctly together, Amory made us see that windmills (I'm simplifying) can provide a couple of times the present level of commodity intensity by the end of this century. He produced a reaction which shocked me. Four people around the place where I was sitting said, 'Now this is a really hopeful message.' I want to set up a situation in which we can get to the core of this issue, because, for me, this is a horrible idea. In some other milieus, Lovins' arguments could be used to increase the expectations of certain establishments who believe that the world will be unviable by the year 2000, and who wish to move towards a viable world of ever more intense social control. What does the politician of self-fulfilling prophecy do? He points out what he sees happening at this very moment and describes it as clearly as possible. He thereby clarifies the issue, perhaps eliminating, to a small degree at least, the possibility of co-optation. When other people begin to see that things really are that way, he can very easily gain their confidence. The danger is that, instead of accepting joyfully and humorously the confidence of others, pointing out that he did not look into the future but only analysed what was quite obvious, such a politician might grab power.

Money is a commodity, what is vernacular?

In my introduction, I said that for Schumacher beauty means a particular appreciation of work and of works that is characteristic to each culture but that rigorously eschews cross-cultural measurement as a margin of preference – cross-cultural measurement by money. I do see that so-called advanced economics now tries increasingly to impute money measurement to vernacular values. For me the funniest of the books is Jerry Baker's *Economics of Marriage*. Jerry Baker has found some seventeen different variables which must be taken into consideration and carefully tracked on curves and in mathematical analyses to reduce sexual relationships between people – their stability, their consequences, their externalities, the profit from them, etc – into a form of economics. One of his pupils has gone one step further, arguing that since masturbation is a preference of some people it therefore must imply some marginality, and a really competent economist should be able to impute to it some money equivalent and thereby add it to the GNP! You have Skolka's papers on the contribution made to the GNP by adding a not yet identified value to the bread picked up in a supermarket, because something happens to it when it is chosen, grabbed and carried, and therefore the bread at home is economically more valuable than the bread on the shelves of a supermarket. In other words, I'm simplifying things and bringing them to an extreme to show the kind of economics against which we have to defend ourselves at this moment.

It is most important to point out that the economic mentality, the attempt at measurement or at operational verification of values, has colonized and finally totally monopolized politics and ethics. We have transformed, in a commodity-centred society, ethics and politics into servants of economics, because we have reduced justice to an equitable or equal distribution of the commodities which we produce. My concern is the decolonization of politics and ethics from economic domination.

John Seymour talks of the British State as 'Nanny'. You are talking about 'mother tongue'. It's tremendous that this gathering has happened but it's not if there isn't a crèche, and claimants can't afford to come. Isn't what you're talking about 'the father tongue'?

You spoke about 'Nanny'; this seems to me a most important thing. Nebrija wrote his grammar in 1492. In 1492 education, *educacion*, *educatio prolis* was a term which didn't exist in English. It is a Latin term, and one which can be predicated only about female subjects. *Educacion*, *educatio prolis* is not something which males – male dogs or male humans, – can do. *Educatio prolis* is the nurturing, the feeding, the warming, the protection which a sow gives to her piglets, which a bitch gives to her puppies, which a mother gives to her *infantes* (non-speakers) who in law are not quite human beings yet.

Males, in Latin from where the word comes, engage in *docentia instructio* (teaching of practical things). Only on rare occasions have I found some example in antiquity, and then it is usually said with a smile that a man is engaged in the *educatio* of somebody. It's like giving birth, something which males don't do. So *educatio* in Latin could not be applied to males. What fascinates me is when did the mentality develop by which male bureaucracies set themselves up as necessary 'nannies' and declared female education activities insufficient for growth into citizenship in a modern state, so making it necessary for people to go through the 'class womb' from which we are born into citizenship?

The reason why this interests me is because I cannot very well avoid speaking about industrial society as a society based on radical uterus envy institutionalized, in which people are assumed to be lifelong children. 'Children' again is a term which has developed only in this period – read Philip Arie's *Centuries of Childhood* – for people who have to be cared for, who have to undergo lifelong education. You show this on your television screens, for England is particularly advanced in this 'nanny' technique by which people have to be carried, transported. People can't simply go any more, they need transportation systems. If people are telefed, they can't participate in any way in the generation of their own food. People have to be cared for, but it is a care which as McKnight says wears the mask of love. This absurd attempt at the creation of a bureaucratic 'Mother' – you used the term 'Nanny' – implies servitude without satisfaction: that is, modernization of poverty or impoverishing enrichment or, as I call it, counter-productive institutional activity. I assume that demand for these services will crash, and then the only question will be 'How shall a politician of self-fulfilling prophecy behave when confronted by a crash which you also see?' If that crash can be avoided, and not just pushed further into the future, let's work at it. But if we come to the conclusion that sooner or later we shall meet that crash, then the most fruitful activity in which we can engage is to figure out how to face it, and whether this is the opening of an entirely new area of hope or whether we must dread it and run away from it.

This is the first time that I have spoken at a paid conference. And I do feel that the moment you have to use a microphone, even with the very good atmosphere that exists here, you inevitably put yourself onto a demagogical platform. It is for this reason that, for the past few years, unless I have to speak with other people I will not use a microphone. I believe that the destruction of the vernacular domain, and therefore the destruction of my certainty that I am the ultimate criterion of how the language has to be spoken, has destroyed also the possibility of scientific research in the vernacular domain, or has very strongly limited it. Science by the people does not mean second level or seventh level incorporation into scientific research hierarchies: it means rethinking the world in terms of my vernacular domain, which by definition is not comparable to yours. This can't be done as long as the ideology of the knowledge stock of a language is permitted among us.

I think any talk about knowledge stock in a meeting such as this should be considered bad taste. It is a phrase which a very famous and very great British economist introduced some fifteen or twenty years ago. It is a profoundly banal concept because it conceives of knowledge as excrement of our minds which can be put together in a heap, or into places called scientific research institutions, where scientists are responsible for making it grow at a certain percentage every year. It is then marketed, channelled through the education system and consumed, incorporated, interiorized by so-called students who are really knowledge consumers or knowledge capitalists. They get knowledge stock-holding certificates.

How can we bring the vernacular?

I tried to describe vernacular language as language that is built out of personal experience. I believe that vernacular language is opposed to taught language. The taught language was as rare in comparison to vernacular language as environmental energy in comparison to muscular energy. There were always some people who cornered the right bend on the river and built a mill there and others who had a big sail on their boat which gave them more power, lifted them above others, but no where near the point to which a man is lifted today by 'hard' energy. The 'soft' energy choice means, not equalization, but rather a step back towards the sail. In the same way there were always, in all cultures, some people who had a taught language, such as the Frankish scribe, the Arabic cadi and the medieval Roman-Latin-speaking chancery officer, but most people were, as in India today, multilingual in several vernaculars.

I learned this in the Sahel. Every village is multilingual. They know Hauser because it's a trade language. They know Bambara because it's the language of half the village. Everbody also knows some Senufo because the other half of the village speaks Senufo; everyone also knows some Arabic for praying purposes; and everybody knows some French for travelling and military purposes. Each of these languages was picked up as a vernacular. In one of these villages I learned the goldsmithing language, not by someone telling me 'this is called thus' but again by observing the master with his pupil speaking about it. I grew into it. In fact, I observe that monolingual populations exist only under three circumstances in the world. Pre-Neolithic tribes, in utter isolation. Second, people who are utterly exploited and marginalized: untouchables in Benares. You may not speak to them and they may not let you know if they understand in Bihari, or in Hindi which is not, precisely, the language they speak. Third, groups which have enjoyed for several generations intensive public or universal schooling. Therefore I say there are two ways one can go about Lovins' soft energy choice. Either say, 'Therefore we now need much more education in order to teach everybody not only how to build a windmill, but also how to build a solar collector'; or say, 'How can we engineer things in such a way that people don't need to be instructed but that the technology becomes transparent?'

What about the people who want to do their own thing?

People who want to do their own thing threaten the job market. They deprive potential workers – administrators, inventors and tax officers – of their jobs. At the moment the total volume of jobs is declining. But economists don't realize this because most of those whose voice is heard have said it will never happen. The service sector is beginning to decline very fast; there's a process of service devolution going on – people learning things on their own. They can look after themselves, they don't need public caretakers or nannies.

With this decline of jobs all the institutionalized agencies, parties, bureaucracies and unions which make a government work are deeply concerned to do everything they can to fight unemployment. The language has not yet been developed by which the interest of the overwhelming majority of people in rendering unemployment useful could be defended. There is still a lack of clear distinction between rights and liberties when jobs are being discussed. This distinction is very clear in the civil rights movement: 'When I claim my liberty to say what I want to say, I'm not stopping or impeding anyone else from saying what they want to say.'

It is very important that this distinction between rights and liberties be introduced when discussing the work-force. This can be done only by political process: we must protect the interest of a nation, of a state, or of a group in maintaining its freedom for useful unemployment. But we still stutter when we have to express this in general political terms. The new politics which wants to protect the right to useful unemployment, which wants to protect the true vernacular domain from any administration of it, and which insists on decentralization rather than on the central, phoney creation of would-be vernacular domains, must stand out of the present political system; because both our opponents are concerned with the growth of commodities, though the Right will be concerned more with growth at all costs and the Left with distribution even if it should hurt growth.

Ivan Illich

Is the community the mainstay of vernacular values?

Some ten years ago, I made a point that any energy invested in transportation which would accelerate any vehicle above 25 k.p.h. would not contribute to time-savings in society but would create entirely new time wastage. I made an odd statement which looked some-what ridiculous, because it was known that progress was tied to mobility levels in society.

There is not one man in any Western country head-ing a department of economics who would not have written during the 1960s at least one paper arguing that the service sector would continue to grow. And there-fore there is no economist around at this moment who is willing to recognize that service devolution is already proceeding very fast. Sociologists now believe that there is absolutely no way back from society to com-munity, if you want to use these two terms. I am asking, 'At which point is community so destroyed through the increase of society that it becomes non-functional and then society itself becomes frustrating because that so-ciety can only go to hell?'

If the state were to abolish compulsory education wouldn't there be a return to child labour?

My goodness, haven't you grown out of 1965? Haven't you read Marx and his statements about child labour? Haven't you read his *Critique of the Gotha Pro-gramme*? You can read about the child labour issue there. I'm against 'childhood'. I am speaking, not for the abolition of school systems, but for their disesta-blishment. Let the people who want them have them, to each his pleasure. Let's do away with children. You don't need them. Children are a bourgeois phenomenon. Childhood as a subculture doesn't exist outside of consumer societies. I can show it to you in a very simple experiment. The Spanish word for child is *niño*. Some years ago I took pictures in the market of Cuernavaca of about 200 people of whom we calculated that 100 were below the age of fourteen. We showed these pictures to people who had gone through High School and they saw about 100 *niños* in these pictures. Then we showed exactly the same pictures to manual labourers, to peasants, to people who had not got very far in school, and they discovered in these pictures five, seven or eight *niños* – those who were dressed up like the doctor's son. For their own young they have much more tender and meaningful words.

What do you think of the media?

I have a brother who, when his children were one or two years old, took them with him from the United States, where he had been living for ten years, to Belgium. I followed the progress of his children in Belgium. They learned French and German, and spoke quite decent English. After they had been back in the United States for about two months I went to visit my brother, and I was struck by the way the two children, by then nine and ten years old, spoke English. It was clearly a delivery and a way of speaking copied from television. That is, even when they spoke to me, they imitated what happens on the screen. So I called my brother and I said to him, 'This is horrible, did you notice it?' And he said, 'Yes, now that you make me think about it. I don't know what to do.' And we calculated that during the summer these children had certainly not spent more than seventy or eighty hours in front of the screen. I believe that in a desirable society network television should not be tolerated. I'm not speaking against the machine itself, there might be some purposes for which somebody would want to use a screen. I have not spoken on television for ten years.

Is the relationship between the reader and writer of a book institutional or vernacular?

I have carefully not opposed 'institutional' to 'vernacular'. I believe that the term 'institution', as used technically, refers to established social habits. There are institutions that are entirely subservient to the vernacular domain. I mentioned some of the key educational ones – sayings, riddles, folk songs, stories – which are incorporated in each vernacular domain, without being schools, for the delivery of a commodity. Therefore I would not oppose vernacular to institutional, but I would oppose vernacular to commercial.

I have been very careful to point out that, in a vernacular society where politics and ethics strengthen the vernacular domain, commodities have a value only if they are tools for vernacular activities. In this sense, I think that the book is one of the most magnificent examples of such a commodity for a vernacular domain. In a media-dominated society, and I know this from my own experience, the book will be treated as a commodity used to destroy the vernacular domain.

The gentleman who asked me the question on education wanted to subject me to an interview. I said to him, 'I have decided that during the rest of my life I shall not give interviews.' So he asked, 'Why do you have a clientele?' I said to him, 'I am a writer, I don't need anybody as an intermediary to say what I really mean.' Once somebody came up to me and said: 'I want an interview with you. Now, Mr Illich, you have published a book, tell us in your own words what you said.'

Most people who write a book have the greatest difficulty in getting it published. The book market at this moment is a pyramid, and as you become more effective as a commodity you have an ethical duty as a writer to abstain, quite consciously, from collaboration in pushing your book. This becomes an increasing responsibility as the book assumes the characteristics of a commodity which is sought not for its content but for its glitter.

Take the two models of opposed institutions, vernacular-oriented institutions and market-oriented institutions: the library and the school. In the library you have random access to use a book as much or as little as you want. The library is a very costly institution, but in comparison to a school system it is nothing. The school system, inevitably, is an institution which spends much more money on capturing its audience than on transmitting to that audience the product which it pretends it is made for. Three months ago I saw a marvellous example, something which really overwhelmed me. I was in Kerala, a southern state of India on the Malabar coast, and I ran into a state-wide village library system. A fully-fledged library must have a minimum of 1,000 books and must prove that during the last year at least 3,000 people took out books. There are 3,500 libraries still waiting for recognition, but there are 4,500 such village libraries around. Many of these libraries are far away from any school. Kerala is also very proud that it has a high rate of literacy. I do not know whether it has schools because it has libraries or libraries because it has schools. The danger now is that with the growth of the school system the library in Kerala will suffer the same fate as English libraries, being viewed by the schoolteacher as a tool where books increasingly are transformed into text books, which I do not consider legitimate books. Text books are teaching tools, they are programme devices – you can even transform Shakespeare into a text book. In fact, for most English speakers it probably is a text book, they have never enjoyed it.

What have you intellectuals got to offer the coal-miners?

I will not be blackmailed by being an intellectual. I have had to repeat this constantly to my Marxist audiences in South America for twenty years. Second, if there's one group I would not trust for social policy discussions, or regard as the most probable source of innovation, it is the unionised workers in the primary sector of industrialised societies. They are, as much as senior company officers, tied to the survival of the hard energy economy.

I want to point out that the soft energy path, which is unavoidable in one form or other, provides us with an entirely new political issue – one that stands at right angles to the politics of growth, of progress, of development in which the Right and the Left have been equally engaged during the last fifty and, particularly, thirty years. The issue is between soft energy as it supports the vernacular domain, and soft energy as the way to make a commodity-intensive society survive.

IV
The Ideal World-View

John Michell

It is a great honour for me to be asked to speak to you; but though I personally feel unworthy of it, I hope you will agree that the subject I am going to speak about is not unworthy of this occasion. For it is a subject of the most vital and immediate interest to all of us. It is about the forms of the future, about the decision, which is within our power, as to the shape of the 'new heaven' and the 'new earth' which necessity demands must be imagined into existence in place of the outworn, obsolescent world-image which reigns so destructively today.

What I am proposing is an inquiry into objective courses, transcending human opinions, from which can be derived a natural philosophy, a humane beneficial way of regarding and relating to the world, capable of uniting those who see the necessity for a new, stable relationship between civilized men and earth, and of effectively challenging the erroneous beliefs and assumptions which are now promoting world annihilation.

I am going to speak about the power of mythology and the influence of the dominant myth on forms of society. And to illustrate what I am talking about, here are two contrasting myths, each one producing an opposite effect on the society that adopts it. First the Newtonian myth: the universe is a great mechanism; see how that prefigured the age of mechanical development in Britain and beyond. Here is another myth, from Plato: 'The world is a living creature.'

Now this second view of the world as an actual living creature, with this earth a living entity, part of a greater living entity; this view is not anti-scientific, nor is it original or eccentric, but, as expressing the consensus of human thought through all ages, it has a better claim to orthodoxy than the materialist myth. That is, people, from their experience, have generally found it more true and more expedient.

In every traditional cosmology, the earth is recognized as a living thing with its own spirit to which people are in some way related. This belief endures throughout the history of philosophy, with Porphyry stating that the physical earth is but the visible form of its real essence, and with the following excellent definition from Banhius Valentinus:

> The earth is not a dead body, but is inhabited by a spirit that is its life and soul. All created things, minerals included, drew their strength from the earth spirit. This spirit is life, it is nourished by the stars and it gives nourishment to all the living things it shelters in its womb. Through the spirit received from on high, the earth hatches the minerals in her womb as the mother her unborn child.

Those were the words of a medieval alchemist, initiate and philosopher, but they might equally well have been spoken by a shaman or elder of a traditional society in any continent on earth. In civilized times when philosophy becomes detached from experience, there are, as we know, occasional outbreaks of the mechanical universe idea. Epicurus tried it out in ancient Greece, and we ourselves are still plagued by bits and pieces from the Newtonian mechanism; but as Schopenhauer put it, "This fundamental error [materialism] . . . raises its head from time to time afresh, until universal indignation compels it to hide itself once more.'

The reason why it is a fundamental error to regard the universe as a mechanism is because of the effects of that view. Science cannot decide the matter one way or the other. If one conceives the universe to be a dead, material creation of physical laws, all experiments will tend to confirm it as such. If one conceives it as a living creature, so it will appear.

Thus, by a decision, we can literally make the world in the image that best suits our interests. The mechanical universe idea was temporarily convenient to an age which was concerned with the development of mechanical inventions. People are always impelled, even unconsciously, to form the human world-order after the model of the universe as they conceive it at the time. Thus the conceptual model of the world, a people's cosmology, has an all-pervading influence on the forms of human life and its institutions. And the reverse is also true. People justify their activities at any time by making a cosmology that reflects their own particular ideas and obsessions.

If we decide to regard the earth as a living creature in an organic universe, that decision will inevitably condition the way we relate to it. The keeper of an animal is careful of the overall health of the creature. If it starts losing hair, or develops skin blemishes or behaves erratically, he will take those as symptoms that all is not well, and that perhaps there is something wrong with his treatment of it. Similarly, if we see the earth as literally a living creature, it takes no specialized knowledge to detect symptoms of overall sickness in its loss of hair through deforestation, skin blemishes in its artificial deserts and despoiled areas of mining and industry, and erratic behaviour in freak weather, the decline or distress of animal species, plagues and diseases in nature and even outbreaks of wars and mass psychosis among people. When it is recognized that all life on earth is one organism together with the parent body, part of the same creature and partaking of the same vital spirit, then it can be seen that sickness in any part symptomizes and causes sickness in the body as a whole.

If we understand that the earth is living, we will naturally relate to it by very different standards from those now obtaining. And our entire mode of science will also be very different. For our interests will be seen to lie, not as now in investigating the physical body of the earth, but in studying its essential spirit, or life force, and the impulses of its nervous system. Thus, out of pure consideration of our own advantage, we shall regain the science which developed from those studies in the past and which sustained the longest-lasting, most stable civilizations of which we have record.

With a promise of returning later to this interesting aspect of the subject, let us now identify the two constant sources from which we naturally derive a cosmology. These two, which are reflections of each other, are human nature and the nature of the universe. They are related to each other, as the ancient philosophers put it, as microcosm to macrocosm. They affect each other, and the reality of our experience is a product of their interactions. Neither human nature nor the universe is conceivable without the other. We cannot think of ourselves other than as part of our surroundings, nor can we observe our universe other than as a projection of ourselves. Hence the absurdity of nineteenth-century science basing itself on the notion that an objective world existed and could be apprehended, independent of our capacity to perceive it. The standards or ideal models behind any sane new world-order must be derived from the nature of human beings and of the universe combined.

That was the synthetic standard that sustained the long-lasting, stable civilizations of antiquity, and the institution which embodied it was the temple or ritual control centre. The ancient temple, of which an example survives in the relics of Stonehenge, was everywhere, it seems, designed in the same way, according to a numerical code of proposition, to express both human and astronomical measurement reconciled in one scheme. From its traditions, and from the archaeological evidence of such examples as the Temple at Jerusalem, it appears that the temple functioned as an instrument of dynamic fusion between the energies of the atmosphere and of the earth. And, as representing both man and universe, it partook of the most obvious quality of both these in that it was cyclical. The rituals performed there varied with the seasons of the year and of the greater astronomical cycles. And it was so designed that different parts of its fabric related to and could be used for observation of the heavenly bodies at different seasons. Then we find astronomical features at Stonehenge in the form of sighting lines to distant markers on the horizon at the rising- or setting-point of sun and moon at the extreme positions of their orbits. Similar astronomical references occur in later temples and Christian churches, an important part of whose function has always been to record times and seasons.

The institution of the temple built like Jerusalem on the Rock of Foundation at the conceptual centre of the world, yet in constant flux through the cycles of ritual performed there; this perfectly expresses the paradox in all human civilizations and settlements: that they are man-made attempts at stability in a world of constant change. Unfortunately for civilization, and disastrously for all tyrants, system-mongers, single-minded utopians and so on, human settlement must to some extent violate human nature which, like the universe, is not a fixed quality, but manifests its different characteristics at different seasons. Edward Carpenter in one of his books with the fine, provocative title *Civilization: its Cause and Cure*, published in 1889, greatly offended his fellow-members of the Fabian Society by referring to civilization as 'a kind of disease which the various races of men have to pass through'. Perhaps that is so. Certainly Genghis Khan believed it when he went through Asia, exterminating cities as being contrary to God's law. According to this view, which is also expressed by several Old Testament prophets, men were made to roam the face of the earth, taking only what nature freely provides, imitating the planets in their regular orbits of their native territory. Settlement, building and agriculture are regarded by nomadic people as sacrilegious, as violations of the goddess or earth spirit. Thus the North American Indian prophet, Smohalla, when the colonists proposed to settle his people in a reservation and turn them into peasants, responded by saying: 'My young men shall never work. Men who work cannot dream, and wisdom comes to us in dreams. You ask me to plough the ground. Shall I take a knife to my mother's breast? You ask me to dig for stone. Shall I dig under her skin for her bones? You ask me to cut grass, but how dare I cut off my mother's hair?'

That sentiment, which has been repeated by aboriginal people all over the world, belongs to the primeval view of the earth as a garden ready planted with all that people could need. That same view is invoked in the classical poets' descriptions of the Golden Age when, as Ovid said, 'People cultivated natural justice of their own accord without need of laws.'

That ideal, anarchistic picture of the Golden Age is always associated with times before civilization, before settlement, when people, travelling in small tribes or family groups, were governed by the movements in the heavens and the progression of the seasons which determined the course of their annual migrations. Human nature was formed in this way and our comparatively few generations of civilized living have not essentially changed it. Yet when we consider this question of the most desirable forms of society in the future, we generally think in terms of a civilization. Very few would seriously advocate a reversal to tribal nomadism. That may, and perhaps inevitably will come about one day, through cataclysm, but obviously it cannot be achieved by planning. What we desire practically is what Plato sensibly called the second best – second best to the precivilized anarchist ideal, the perfect form of Golden Age in which everyone acts naturally in accordance with everyone else. This second best, which is a just, stable, self-perpetuating civilization is, says Plato, virtually as good as the first, if properly founded and maintained.

The understanding that human nature is still the nature of the primeval nomad gives us insight into the causes of failure of so many utopias, new republics, ideal societies and self-regulating communities over, say, the last 400 years. Most of these have been based on someone's plausible idea at the time (i.e. Marxism) or someone's moral prejudices, as in Puritanism, or someone's religious cult, or on naive hopes that people of goodwill can get on and function well together in an unstructured but settled community. All these are based on partial or erroneous apprehensions of human nature. People cannot for ever be fixed in one state of mind, nor can we accept for long any particular moral ideals or man-made cults. Human nature is fluctuating and cyclical and some of its many sides are rationally irreconcilable with others. Thus no society which is based on entirely rational or single-minded principles can endure for any great length of time.

The best that can be achieved by way of a society that reflects and responds to human nature is one in which the various aspects of our nature are each allowed seasonal expression. Plato gives a clue to how this is achieved when he says that the colonists of his new republic should take over both the sites and the dates of traditional local festivals and so arrange it that there are at least 365 festivals in the course of a year. Thus the primeval journey is ritualized both physically with processions and pilgrimages to the various sites of traditional sanctity, and mentally through experience of the different states of mind celebrated at each festival.

Festivals, originating in the Ancient World, which celebrated irrational, anti-authoritarian states of mind, survived in Europe into the Middle Ages, including feast days when for twenty-four hours the youngest or most worthless citizens ruled the city, during which time their decrees, however foolish, had the force of law. These were, unwisely in the long run, suppressed by humourless Church authorities, and at the Reformation the Puritans put down many other festivals because they celebrated human attributes which were morally disapproved of, such as sexuality, intoxication and the worship of nature. Thus many sides of humanity, denied lawful seasonal expression, were left to assume ugly, anti-social forms.

We began by initiating an enquiry into the social forms of the future: how we can determine them by the cosmology, or understanding of the world, we choose to adopt, and where we should look for standards and principles in forming this new cosmology.

It is an ambitious programme to undertake in one hour, but the subject is the most important one to raise in this present company, because the issue behind it is immediate and urgent.

It seems to me that there are at present two general world-views or cosmologies, one established in power, and the other, still in the process of formation, which is emerging to challenge it.

The force which is now dominant in most of the centres of power throughout the world uses the expanding universe theory of modern cosmology, linked with social applications of Darwinism, as the model for an apes-to-spaceman view of history, according to which our generation has achieved the climax of all previous science because we are for the first time, though at the cost of a vast proportion of the world's resources, in a position to explore the extra-terrestrial universe. There is official talk of mining other planets, of space colonies and so on – all of which ignores the fact that our human nature was formed here on this earth, that here is the climate and scale of things for which we have been designed, together with all the sensory delights we have been equipped to experience, and that this earth is our own paradise.

It is evident, therefore, that any philosophy which advocates the continued rape of this earth, our potential paradise, in the hope of achieving some kind of man-made paradise among alien planets, is a philosophy that is inimical to human interests because it threatens the very existence of our living earth. No sane person would propose such a thing, yet that very proposal, to extend our devastation of this planet to others, to start colonies or life-craft in space, is actually put forward by certain powerful technological institutions. These institutions depend for their existence on encouragement and finance from governments of large, wealthy, politically centralized states or from the transnational business corporations. And here we must consider the political consequences of the cosmology now dominant, which may prove quite as menacing as its physical effects. I am referring to the tendency, inherent in the expanding universe cosmology, of the centres and institutions of political and economic power to become not only larger but more unified and more like each other. It is not necessary to subscribe to theories of a universal conspiracy, which now seem, not surprisingly, to be returning to fashion, to become aware of the looming spectre of a one-world system of government, a parody of the brotherhood-of-man vision of idealists and utterly opposed to it in spirit. The form of such a system would no doubt be a duality of powers like two magnetic poles, each representing a rival economic theory, but both united by one basic view of the world, and neither allowing any serious challenge to the cosmological consensus.

That state of affairs is now so clearly in prospect that it is urgent for us to be aware of its consequences. Schumacher is among many who have pointed out that the larger the system the more mediocre, the closer to the lowest common denominator, become its rulers and its ruling philosophy. The thing is no longer under intelligent human control, but as a blind force reacts with its rival force in accordance with the rules of the game for which both have been programmed. Thus the two rivals in the world-power game continue, uninhibited by human reason, to compete for the world's remaining mineral resources and the allegiance of its helot population, for dominance of outer space and other fatuous, suicidal objectives.

Now, it seems to me that there is but one way in which this looming vision of the future may be dispelled. It is by destroying the source of power that fuels the growth of our present political and economic institutions – that is, by challenging the myths that support them. I am speaking of cosmological revolution, of the formation and growth to the status of accepted orthodoxy of a new world-view that must of necessity replace the one now dominant.

We live now within a basically material, ever-expanding universe, for that is the dominant myth of astronomers today. And related to that myth are many others which developed in the course of recent history and have grown together to form the Great Myth, the structure of orthodox beliefs that informs all influential systems of education, politics and economics. Examples of elements in the Great Myth include the theory of human progress to which some scholars attribute origins in early Christianity, when the pagan belief in the cyclical nature of redemption or renewal of culture was replaced by the idea of Christ as a once-and-for-all redeemer who introduced humanity to a higher level of consciousness, transcending that of the Ancients.

The myth of history as progress, with its overtones of a religious faith, justified religious and economic imperialism, by which the benefits of a moral religion and an economic system reflecting the primacy of matter were urged with missionary zeal on tradionalist native societies. This myth both inspired and drew credibility from Darwin's postulation of a hierarchy among species, with man at the peak of an evolutionary order of creatures, and, by an extraordinary chance, Darwin himself, representing the modern, rational man of science, at its very apex.

Darwin was of a generation which believed, almost without question, that Christian, scientific civilization was superior in quality to any other, present or past. And to that prejudice he gave what appeared to be scientific sanction with his borrowed phrase, 'The survival of the fittest.' That phrase amounted to a death sentence on traditionalist native people in many parts of the world, for it was seen as implying that, since they had taken no part in the development of modern scientific consciousness, they had been left behind in the struggle to be the fittest, and their races were, therefore, doomed by natural law to be supplanted by more vigorous, more inventive cultures. Karl Marx, who also saw history as a struggle for power, offered to dedicate *Das Kapital* to Darwin; and Hitler, a confirmed Darwinian, acted quite logically in terms of his belief when he undertook to make his people the fittest and most dominant at the expense of others. Recently and significantly, when the Communists took over China, the first new text introduced to all schools was not Marx or Lenin but Darwin. Mr Heath, when he visited China as Prime Minister, was told that an acceptable gift for Chairman Mao would be a first edition of Darwin's *Origin of Species*. Darwinism has been found as supportive of scientific atheism as of capitalist expansion. To become aware of the intensity of official promotion of evolution theory, take a look at the current list of BBC publications and note the number of titles that are straight Darwin propaganda.

This is not the occasion to attempt criticism of Darwinism as a biological theory, and here I shall merely note that whereas in Darwin's time geology was in such a primitive state that he could blame 'gaps in the fossil record' for its failure to provide evidence of the missing links he expected to find among species, despite a century and more of intense research there has still not been discovered a chain of links between any two species; and indeed the one bit of evidence which finally convinced waverers that Darwin was right about human descent, the Piltdown skull, turned out to be an evolutionists' forgery.

But, although many biologists are now questioning Darwin's notion on the grounds that it is incompatible with the phenomena of life as they observe it, the effects of Darwinism, and the reasons for my objections to it, are far deeper than merely academic. For his view of life as a spontaneous development from simple organisms to larger, more complex forms has been taken as a universal paradigm, used to justify similar development in political and economic contexts. And when we consider the effects of Darwinism, as already mentioned, in providing what amounted to a tyrants' and racists' charter, we may feel inclined to take another look at a rival of Darwin, the saintly Kropotkin.

There has been much speculation as to what extent the fact of Darwin being a sickly, low-spirited man who saw life as a struggle contributed towards his making 'the survival of the fittest' the first principle in nature. Kropotkin disputed the very basis of Darwinism, and said that, on the contrary, nature's first principle is mutual aid. Relationships between and within species are not primarily aggressive but co-operative. It is not so much a matter of struggle as of symbiosis. Nature is one creature, its various parts corresponding subtly and beneficially with all others.

Now the distinction between these two fundamental views and the difference between their social effects are very striking indeed. And with Kropotkin we come to the positive side of this enquiry, to consider the forms and effects of the ideal world-view to replace the present orthodoxy.

Behind Kropotkin's mutual aid is the idea of a

steady-state universe. As we know, astronomers for ever dispute about the reigning principle of motion – whether the universe is eternally expanding, or breathing in and out like a creature, or in a state of dynamic equilibrium. Most of us are in no position to judge between the rival schools of astronomers. In their science, as in all others, there operates the law, as enunciated by Charles Fort, that 'for every expert there is an equal and opposite expert'. We are quite free, therefore, to approach the matter another way and to choose whatever view of the universe best suits our interests.

We have now had a long enough experience of expanding-universe cosmology to be well aware of the one-sidedness of its values – its encouragement of growth and innovation and its respect for the quality of inventiveness above that of traditional craftsmanship. The unassimilated changes taking place in our time are causing a popular reaction in favour of stability, with the odd result that quite recent periods, which, we know, fell very short of any Golden Age ideal, are being invested with that image by the transmuting force of nostalgia. We are frequently warned about the dangers of millenial thinking or yearning for the ideal; and it is indeed dangerous both to the present order of authority and in itself as tending to produce outbreaks of mass psychosis, such as the mad, bloody affair of the Anabaptist republic of New Jerusalem in sixteenth-century Münster. Yet the tendency in human nature to look backwards to a past Golden Age and forward to its future restoration is as old as history. And though it has often been misdirected by mad, ignorant or excitable people, it is potentially a most valuable element in our psychological make-up, for it represents an idealism which ultimately may be the salvation of our human race.

A steady-state cosmology, and its social correspondence, a settled, civilized state in which the terrestrial paradise is realized and the ideal is aspired to here and now, the dream-like qualities of stability, justice and harmony which characterized the Golden Age – we may never quite achieve all that, but, as Plato said, since people need a goal or a model to live up to, it might as well be the best and highest that can be conceived.

Start to adopt the steady-state view of reality, based on the idea of constant, though cyclically fluctuating, rather than evolutionary human nature, and of a universe which, at least as far as we are concerned, is constant and eternal. Start, as many of you have done, to look at things this way, and one's whole view of history, our relationship to the universe and the limitations and proper aims of civilization and science suffer a profound sea-change, which puts one quite out of sympathy with the doctrines of the Great Myth as propounded in colleges and practised in government.

History, for example. It is important for the sustenance of the Great Myth that history should illustrate the 'rise of man' idea, with our civilization as unique and representing a new level of human consciousness and achievement. So our British history, as generally taught, begins with the imperialist Romans. Before then, the inhabitants of these islands are pictured as historically irrelevant barbarians, even though the contemporary records of Caesar and other writers deny it, even though archaeology now attributes a profound, universally-linked culture to the builders of Stonehenge and contemporary structures, and even though old chroniclers list and describe Kings of England going back hundreds of years BC. These last have been arbitrarily blotted out of the record as legendary, with the implication of imaginary, because our early histor-

ical knowledge of them came through oral bardic traditions which were always carefully preserved and
handed down, rather than through contemporary do-
cuments, necessarily non-existent.

Thus we are left with a history curtailed and muti-
lated by the requirements of the Great Myth. And the
Americans are in a worse state, their history beginning
conventionally with the European colonies. Compare
the traditional histories of the East which take wide
sweeps thousands of years into the past and record,
not a rise, but a decline of culture from times of legendary sage rulers and long-lasting civilizations.

For pragmatic reasons it is in our interest to adopt
a longer view of history that we may see more clearly
the nature of our civilization and develop a coherent
critique of its aberrant aspects. To do so is merely to
return to the earlier mode of historical orthodoxy.
Plato followed the custom of antiquity when he referred to the greater wisdom of past ages, and to a
great, widespread and ultimately self-destroying civilization in his history of Atlantis.

If, as I believe many of us are unconsciously finding
it necessary to do, we look at history in a far wider
context than the present literal–material mode allows,
we find that overall it records tides of civilization – not
a one way progression from nomadic hunters to scholars and scientists, but a fluctuation between these two
states.

We should recognize, therefore, that inventiveness
and the urge to elaborate artificial societies are not the
only sides of our nature that contribute towards a balanced civilization. Paradoxically, those elements in
ourselves which urge us to renounce civilization and
resume the life-style of natural primeval man also need
recognition.

I spoke earlier of Plato's recipe, following traditional

practice, of a round of festivals to celebrate the anti-authoritarian sides of our nature. The study of long-lasting civilizations in the past shows that only in this way, by allowing society to reflect the entirety of human nature, not merely its positive, inventive aspect, but its traditionalist, earth-rooted aspect also, can we hope to slow down and humanize the inevitable tendency to rise and dissolve which is inherent in all human institutions, the greatest civilizations included.

I should like to consider an aspect of this subject which has intrigued many of us. If we adopt a steady-state model of the universe, as did the most enduring of ancient civilizations, the type of science appropriate to the steady-state society will be very different from science as it is now, for its aims will be different. All over the world there are traditions and substantial relics of an ancient system of science which, because its aims were so totally different from our own, has been utterly misunderstood by modern scholars. The purpose of a steady-state science is to form relationships between people and human activities and the world we live in. Thus, ancient civilizations were deeply concerned with timekeeping and with the astrological influences of time on human psychology. For that they concentrated much on astronomy.

Recent studies of stone circles and other prehistoric sites have revealed the remarkable accuracy with which their builders were able to observe and mark the seasons of the solar and lunar year and the eclipse cycle. Yet astronomy and timekeeping were only part of their function. There are features of these sites, including their interrelations and their connection with geological faults and underground water, which accord with the universal traditions surrounding the old stones in indicating that they were used as instruments of an alchemical science to do with procuring a creative fusion between the natural forces of earth and sky. Three general types of use for these instruments are suggested by their legends: for increasing the fertility of the land and living things, for healing, and for inspiring oracles and prophecy. It was, in short, the science of a settled agricultural people who were concerned to augment the gifts of nature, both physical and spiritual, while keeping themselves and their communities in contact with the vital forces of the universe.

A fundamental way in which the ancient science differs from our own is that it was not intended to represent progress, but was regarded more as a compensation. In all traditional histories, such as those of the Chinese and Ancient Greeks already referred to, the remote ancestors were thought of as wiser and more knowledgeable than the present generation because they were able to live more simply, without the elaborate institutions of civilization. Science was seen as the compensation by weaker generations for the lost classic style of the Ancients. Thus its purpose was not to progress but to delay and make up for regression. The old perception is that cultures do not develop gradually through unaided human efforts, but are created at their highest at the start of one of those mysterious cycles of earth-renewal, influx of cosmic energy or whatever, which result in the appearance of godlike individuals or culture heroes who establish the new order of the age. From that time entropy takes over and a people's culture begins its long decline. Religion and science are developed with the object of arresting that decline by keeping society in touch with its cultural origins through the perpetuation of customs and rituals. When these become mere empty forms, when the knowledge and perception behind them are lost, the society is in its period of decadence, and its end comes either by gradual dissolution or catastrophe.

The Ancients were well aware of these cycles and studied them closely in order to attempt the orderly progression of civilizations, each one lasting without disruption through its alloted span. With this idea in their minds, the Chinese until quite recently did everything they could to discourage social innovations and disruptive inventions. And since they reckoned that the merchant class were the most likely to attempt innovations that would be to their own advantage and nobody else's (see, for example, what forces are pressing for universal metrication today), the Chinese rulers were reluctant to abolish all bandits from the paths of commerce, for their activities tended to prevent merchants from becoming too rich. And if a merchant should become so rich that he aspired to become a member of a higher class, the only accepted superior life-style was that of a retired scholar. Thus the tendency of big businessmen to persuade governments to promote their interests at the expense of everyone else's was considerably mitigated.

The traditional view of the life-span of a culture as a process of running down from the time of original inspiration is the opposite of the modern view. The idea that cultures tend naturally to improve and develop is related to the Darwinian belief that life-forms have spontaneously organized themselves from simpler to more complicated organisms, with human awareness somehow developing as a function of matter.

This general notion has been criticized as contradicting the second law of thermodynamics, the one that speaks of entropy as a first principle, the tendency of energy to spread itself out and dissipate. And a more direct challenge to Darwinian orthodoxy is now being mounted by the biologists. They observe that comparatively short periods, indicated by the fossil record, between the disappearance of one species and the appearance of others are far *too* short to be compatible with classic evolutionism. No doubt in time, since ideas themselves are cyclical, we shall find the scientific justification for some form of the traditional creation myth – that both life-forms and cultures are products of certain creative periods or events, however explained, and that their life-spans thereafter are determined by the force of entropy.

One of the best available sources for a study of the ancient science is the relic of it that has survived among the Chinese, which they call 'feng-shui'. This traditional science was utterly misvalued by Westerners until quite recently, and the reason why now at last many people are beginning to take a serious interest in it and in the principles of co-operation with nature that lie behind it is, I suggest, because the need for some such system – or, at the very least, for the attitude to life it reflects – is now becoming evident.

Feng-shui is a product of that way of looking at things that I have called steady-state cosmology. Behind it is the idea that the primeval earth is the paradise from which, by settlement, we have become alienated; but that this alienation may be mitigated by planning our settled communities and their environments as types of artificial paradise, following the patterns of the original. Feng-shui provides a code for landscape and building design. Its practitioners, by means of a magnetic compass and by astronomical and other criteria, determine the correct position and shape of all human additions to the landscape from tombs and temples to houses and watercourses. They are trained to detect the invisible paths of vital magnetic currents through the earth's surface, which they see as corresponding to the lines and centres of subtle energy which Chinese medicine recognizes in the human body. And they take into account the strength, direction and seasonal quality of the landscape currents in deciding what locations are suitable for what purposes.

Feng-shui has degenerated in modern times into a magical system for bringing good luck, but its influence when it was practised as a state science under the direct patronage of the Emperor can be seen in the wonderfully harmonious landscape of old China, in which groups of buildings are placed in relationship with their natural surroundings by the same rules of composition that are followed by traditional Chinese painters. And although the classic Chinese landscape with its temples, pavilions, feng-shui masts and other such apparatus may seem to us more romantic than practical, these arrangements served in fact a highly practical purpose, and the subject is therefore highly relevant to our present enquiry. For the effect of feng-shui on the country and its people was to create what was described by Professor Abercrombie, the great post-war authority on town and country planning, as 'the most elaborate landscape which has ever existed, and landscape which had to preserve certain spiritual values and also to fulfil the practical purpose of supporting a dense population.'

See how that last statement contradicts the assumption of people who believe that the first, most important step to world sanity is to reduce our population. Those who are emphatic about this issue see people as being in general destructive of their natural surroundings. And that, of course, under the present conditions of alienation between people and landscape, is quite true. But in steady-state society the opposite is true: the more dense and varied the population, within obvious, natural limits, the better worked and more productive becomes the countryside and the more refined and civilized the landscape. It is not the size of the population that determines whether a country is ruined or made prosperous, but the way in which that population relates to its surroundings. The old Chinese landscape which looked as was intended, so natural and undisturbed, was actually to a great extent artificially composed. Hills were raised, river courses and the shapes of mountains altered in accordance with the rules of feng-shui and the flow of earth energies as directed by it. And the pagodas and pavilions, so authentically placed on rocks and mountains, were designed practically to temper these energies to the advantage of human settlements and the fertility of the land.

Every country in the world shows evidence that a local science with similar aims and methods to those of Chinese feng-shui once flourished there. Our European megaliths seem to correspond in function to the later, more elaborate monuments of China. No doubt it will not be long before we know more about this almost forgotten universal science. Active research into this intriguing subject is rapidly growing. Some of you will have heard of the Dragon Project, organized by the *Ley Hunter* magazine, which has a group of scientists and dowsers engaged in investigating and measuring the seasonal flux of the earth energies detected at stone circles and other such sites. The importance of all this, as I see it, is that we are being impelled, semi-consciously and by the necessity of the present situation, to think about sources of natural power which are different in quality and in their social implication from the power-sources now monopolized by central governments and big business groups. It suggests that a new mode of perception is arising which may, and I think must, revolutionize the entire world-order that obtains today.

Now it is time to sharpen the points already made and, perhaps, in conclusion, to take the matter a little further. The world today is dominated by ideas and forces which are inimical to its survival. The great modern institutions of power, as is the tendency of all human institutions, have gained independent momentum beyond rational human control, and, since any institution is more stupid and stubborn than any of the individuals who compromise it, they cannot go against their own programmes by abolishing themselves or reforming their own destructive characters. It seems that we are in the power of forces which we or our ancestors first set in motion but which have become blind and inhuman, destined to react with each other in swings of ever greater violence until they destroy for ever the precarious balance between the interests of civilization and those of nature. In terms of our present mode of reasoning it seems that nothing can avert, or even long delay, the cataclysmic demise of ourselves and our native planet.

But the forces and institutions that seem so unchallengeably dominant today have one point of vulnerability. They are the creatures of our collective view of the world, and their continued existence depends on that view of the world being maintained. Any cosmology is successful only to the extent that it reflects the world we know and experience. And the cosmology still dominant has revealed an obvious flaw which must in time prove fatal. It no longer accords with scientific perception. Physics, which was once thought capable of discovering the material basis of the universe, has instead discovered that there is no matter. The phenomena of sub-atomic physics are not tiny, indivisible particles, which is the belief on which all schools of materialism have based their faith, but rather an affair of dynamic relationships. The infinitesimal world consists of certain dynamic types which can only be expressed through the relationships of number. Thus we find confirmation for the very ancient doctrine that the universe developed through a pre-existant code of number, which is why the whole of nature exhibits permutations of a limited number of geometric types, static and dynamic.

This must have a radical influence on cosmology. The universe is not an affair of particles forming themselves into dense, permanent clusters, ever more organized, but of ever-fluctuating relationships, defined and limited by the laws of number and proportion. Thus the old Chinese landscape, with the nodes of its energy structure marked by masts and pagodas to create a placid magnetic field, is a truer representation of the real world than is the megalomaniac headquarters of an expanding business corporation.

When we think of future societies we must, if we are correctly to reflect the order of the universe, think in terms of dynamic geometry, that is of types of harmony within societies and between them and their surroundings. And if that sounds a bit general, let us consider one aspect of civilized relationships, that between people and power-centre.

All of us in our time have seen a phenomenal growth in the world centres of power, the growth of political, industrial and social centres, and the way in which the big centres increasingly draw power from provincial and independent centres, all tending towards that one-world system of authority that I have already spoken of. Now to deflate this process we must understand the dynamic of centres and what they mean.

Nomadic people recognize some rock or landscape as the sacred centre of their territory; settled people have some form of omphalos stone to mark their world centre, and that in time becomes the place of the temple, the market, the academy and the various central institutions of civilization. I wonder if the space-colony fanatics ever consider how it is that in prehistoric times parts of the country we now find barely inhabitable – the Hebridean Islands, for example – were not only densely populated but enjoyed a local culture which from its surviving mythology appears to have been as high and heroic as that of the ancient Isles of Greece. It was because their local centres held. The megalith builders practised a science that was virtually universal. This we know from the indentical units of measurements in monuments from Britain to Japan and, as is now reported, in South America. Yet that science was everywhere adapted to local conditions and controlled by local communities. Thus people were not drawn to large, distant power-centres; culture and power were locally generated. One lived at the centre of one's own universe with the conception that the world's wisest men were in one's own community.

How can would-be social reformers take practical steps towards reversing the culture drain? How can one act, within the bounds of what is legal and practical, to restore culture and independence to local communities within a system that is programmed not to tolerate such rivalry? Well, I am no prophet, except occasionally, like all of us, to amuse our friends. And even after years of brain-racking, these are questions that I cannot answer. But even for amusement I do not play the prophet of doom. For they say that every great change comes about through changes in individuals. In the near quarter-century since I was at college I have seen so many changes in common perception and patterns of thought, together with a revival of ideas from old philosophies long thought moribund, that the possibility of cosmological revolution and the dethroning of the Great Myth no longer seems a remote one. You remember how in Revelation the 'new heaven and new earth' that appears in Chapter 21 is not a creation of man-made utopian schemes but a pre-existent pattern, divinely revealed. And its manifestation, the New Jerusalem, symbol of true philosophy and a corresponding harmonious human order, is, I believe, something that occurs to our minds at different periods of history. It is an archetypal pattern with roots deep in human nature which becomes manifest through a certain way of thought or ideal philosophy. It is that philosophy, and its social implications, that I have been attempting this afternoon to introduce as the best possible alternative to the Great Myth that dominates our present civilization. And I will end with the words used by Thomas Taylor, the heroic early nineteenth-century Platonist, to characterize this life-saving philosophy. 'It is,' he said, 'coeval with the universe itself. And however its continuity may be broken by opposing systems, it will make its reappearance at different periods of time as long as the sun shall continue to illuminate the earth.'

V
Buddhist Physics

Fritjof Capra

In 1973, while I was working on *The Tao of Physics* which is, in a sense, a book about Buddhist physics, I read in the *Guardian* that somebody had written a book about Buddhist economics. I was very intrigued by that and I wanted to read the book which was, of course, E. F. Schumacher's *Small is Beautiful*. I did not buy the book right away, because I could not afford the hardcover price and had to wait until it came out in paperback. But from that time on I felt there was some kinship between Schumacher's ideas and my own. This feeling has grown stronger after reading *Small is Beautiful* and meeting Fritz Schumacher, and I am delighted and honoured to have this opportunity today to show you the connection between *Small is Beautiful* and *The Tao of Physics*. This connection has, in fact, generated a new book, on which I am still working and of which this lecture will be a kind of summary.

To convey the basic theme of my current work, I shall begin by making a few comments about the evolution of our civilization.

Even the casual observer of our cultural evolution cannot fail to notice the striking disparity between the development of intellectual power, scientific knowledge and technological skills, on the one hand, and of wisdom, spirituality and ethics, on the other. Scientific and technological knowledge have grown exponentially ever since the Greeks embarked on the scientific venture in the sixth century BC. During these twenty-five centuries, there has hardly been any progress in the conduct of social affairs. The spirituality and moral standards of Lao Tzu or Buddha – who also lived in the sixth century BC – were clearly not inferior to ours. They marked a culmination of spiritual development, rather than the beginning of an ascending curve.

Human progress, then, has been a purely rational and intellectual affair, and this one-sided evolution has now reached a highly alarming stage; a situation so paradoxical that it borders insanity. We have piled up tens of thousands of nuclear weapons; enough to destroy the entire world several times over. At the same time, we are busy manufacturing equally dangerous nuclear power plants producing massive quantities of radioactive waste that threaten to extinguish life on our planet.

Even without the threat of a nuclear catastrophe, the global ecosystem and the further evolution of life on earth are seriously endangered and may well end in a large-scale ecological disaster. Our prodigious technology does not seem to be of any help. We can control the soft landings of spacecraft on distant planets, but we are unable to control the polluting fumes emanating from our cars and factories. We are promised the perfect life in gigantic space colonies, but still cannot manage our cities. Meanwhile, the business world makes us believe that huge industries producing pet foods and cosmetics are a sign of our high standard of living, while economists try to tell us that we cannot 'afford' adequate health care, education, or public transport.

All this suggests a profound imbalance in our culture – in our thoughts and feelings, our values and attitudes, and our social and political structures. Further reflection shows that the roots of this cultural crisis lie in the imbalance between two modes of consciousness which have been recognized as characteristic aspects of human nature throughout the ages. They are usually called the rational and intuitive modes, or the scientific and religious modes, and have also been described by various other terms – masculine/feminine, linear/non-linear, and so on. The Chinese have called them the *yang* and the *yin*, and they never saw them as experiences belonging to separate categories, but always as two sides of the same reality; extreme parts of a single whole. In the traditional Chinese view, all manifestations of reality, including the manifestations of human nature, are generated by the dynamic interplay between these two polar forces. According to an ancient Chinese text,

> The *yang* having reached its climax retreats in favour of the *yin*;
> the *yin* having reached its climax retreats in favour of the *yang*.

It is very instructive to observe the attitudes of our culture with regard to these complementary aspects of human nature. The *yang* aspect is our masculine side – the active, rational, competitive, scientific side. The *yin* aspect is our feminine side – the yielding, intuitive, co-operative, mystical side. Our society has consistently favoured the *yang* over the *yin*: activity over contemplation, rational knowledge over intuitive wisdom, science over religion, competition over co-operation, etc.

Furthermore, instead of recognizing that the personality of each man and of each woman is the result of an interplay between feminine and masculine elements, we have established a static, rigid order where all men are supposed to be masculine and all women feminine, and we have given men the leading roles and most of society's privileges.

However, I believe that we are now witnessing the beginning of a tremendous evolutionary movement. As the Chinese text says, the *yang*, having reached its extreme, retreats in favour of the *yin*. The sixties and seventies have generated a whole series of philosophical, religious and political movements which all seem to go in the same direction. The rising concern with ecology, the strong interest in mysticism, the rediscovery of holistic approaches to health and healing, and – perhaps most important of all – the rising feminist awareness, are all manifestations of the same evolutionary trend. They all counteract the overemphasis of rational, masculine attitudes and values, and attempt to regain a balance between the masculine and feminine sides of human nature.

I shall argue that physicists can make a valuable contribution to overcoming the current cultural imbalance. Ever since the seventeenth century, physics has been the shining example of an 'exact' science, and has served as the model for all the other sciences. For two and a half centuries, classical physics developed a mechanistic view of the world, seeing the universe as a mechanical system composed of elementary building blocks. The other sciences accepted this view as the correct description of reality and modelled their own theories accordingly.

In the twentieth century, however, physics went through several conceptual revolutions which clearly revealed the limitations of the mechanistic world-view and led to an organic, ecological view of the world which shows great similarities to the views of mystics of all ages and traditions. The universe is no longer seen as a machine made up of a multitude of separate objects, but appears as a harmonious, indivisible whole; a network of dynamic relationships that include the human observer and his or her consciousness in an essential way.

The fact that modern physics, the manifestation of an extreme specialization of the rational mind, is now making contact with mysticism, the essence of religion and the manifestation of an extreme specialization of the intuitive mind, shows very beautifully the unity and complementary nature of the rational and intuitive modes of consciousness. Physicists, therefore, can provide a scientific basis for the change in attitudes and values that our culture needs so urgently in order to survive. Modern physics can show the other sciences that scientific thinking does not necessarily have to be reductionist and mechanistic; that holistic and ecological views are also scientifically sound.

I shall first outline the world-view of classical physics and its influence on the other sciences, and shall then discuss some of the basic concepts of twentieth-century physics and their implications for science and society.

The Mechanistic Newtonian World-View

The world-view of classical physics, which could also be called the traditional Western world-view, has its roots in the philosophy of the Greek atomists who saw matter as being made of several basic building blocks, the atoms, which are purely passive and intrinsically dead. They were thought to be moved by external forces which were often assumed to be of spiritual origin, and thus fundamentally different from matter.

This image became an essential part of the Western way of thinking. It gave rise to the dualism between spirit and matter, between the mind and the body, which is characteristic of Western thought. This dualism was formulated in its sharpest form in the philosophy of Descartes who based his view of nature on a fundamental division into two separate and independent realms: that of mind (*res cogitans*), and that of matter (*res extensa*). The Cartesian division allowed scientists to treat matter as dead and completely separate from themselves, and to see the material world as a multitude of different objects assembled into a huge machine. Such a mechanistic view was held by Newton who constructed his mechanics on its basis and made it the foundation of classical physics.

The mechanistic view of nature is closely related to a rigorous determinism. The giant cosmic machine was seen as being completely causal and determinate; all that happened had a definite cause and gave rise to a definite effect. The philosophical basis of this strict determinism was the fundamental division between the I and the world introduced by Descartes. As a consequence of this division, it was believed that the world could be described objectively, i.e. without ever mentioning the human observer, and such an objective description of nature became the ideal of all science.

Influence of the Newtonian Model on Other Sciences

From the second half of the seventeenth century to the end of the nineteenth, the mechanistic Newtonian model of the universe dominated all scientific thought. The natural sciences, as well as the humanities and social sciences, all modelled themselves after Newtonian physics, and many of them hold on to this model even now that physicists have gone far beyond it.

Before discussing the impact of Newtonian physics on other fields, I want to make an important point.

The new conception of the universe that has emerged from modern physics does not mean that Newtonian physics is wrong, or that our current theories are right. We have come to realize in modern science that all our theories are approximations to the true nature of things. Each theory is valid for a certain range of phenomena. Beyond this range, it no longer gives a satisfactory description of nature and new theories have to be found to replace it – or, better, to extend it by improving the approximation.

The question, then, will be: how good an approximation is the Newtonian model as a basis for the other sciences? In physics itself, it had to be abandoned at the level of the very small (in atomic and subatomic physics) and at the level of the very large (in astrophysics and cosmology). In other fields, the limitations may be of a different kind. It should be noticed that what we are talking about is not so much the application of Newtonian physics to other phenomena but rather the application of the mechanistic and reductionist world-view on which Newtonian physics is based. It will be necessary for each science to find out where the limitations of this world-view lie in a particular context.

Biology and Medicine

In biology, the Newtonian model led to the idea that a living organism could be regarded as a machine constructed from separate parts. Such a mechanistic biology was first expounded by Descartes and has dominated the life sciences up to the present day. The machine analogy suggests that living organisms can be understood by taking them to pieces and trying to put them together again from the knowledge of their parts.

This approach, indeed, still constitutes the backbone of most contemporary biological thinking.

The mechanical models of biology had a strong influence on medicine which has come to regard the human body as a machine that can be analysed in terms of its parts. Disease is seen as an outside entity that invades the body and attacks a particular part. The doctor's role is to intervene, either physically (through surgery) or chemically (through drugs) and to treat the afflicted part, different parts being treated by different specialists.

To associate a particular illness with a definite part of the body is, of course, very useful in many cases. But Western medicine has overemphasized this reductionist approach and has developed its specialized disciplines to a point where doctors are no longer able to view disease as a disturbance of the whole organism, nor to treat it as such. What they do is treat a particular part of the body, and this is generally done without taking the rest of the body into account – let alone considering the psychological and social aspects of the patient's illness.

Psychology

Classical psychology, like classical physics, is based on the Cartesian divisions between the *res cogitans* and the *res extensa*. Based on this division, two approaches have been developed to study the mind. Behaviourism chose to study the effects of mind on matter by studying behaviour, and applied the methodology of classical physics to this task. Psychological phenomena were reduced to psychic building blocks and were related to physiological stimuli which were assumed to be their causes. As in classical biology, living organisms were seen as machines that react to external stimuli, and this stimulus-response mechanism was modelled after Newtonian physics.

Behaviourists, who still constitute the mainstream of academic psychology, defend their approach by claiming that it is the only scientific approach to psychology, thus clearly identifying the reductionist, mechanistic framework with science.

Freud started from the other side of the Cartesian division. Instead of just studying behaviour, he chose to study the *res cogitans* itself through introspection. Although not dealing with matter, he nevertheless wanted to develop a scientific psychology, and to do so he established a conceptual relationship between psycho-analysis and classical physics.

Like physicists, Freud searched for basic building blocks. He focussed on basic instincts and postulated the ego, id and super-ego as basic psychological structures, located and extended in psychological space. These structures are seen as some kind of internal objects which are in conflict. The mechanism and machineries of the mind are all driven by forces modelled after Newtonian mechanics.

Economics

From psychology I shall now turn to the social sciences and, in particular, to economics. Present-day economics, like most social sciences, is fragmentary and reductionist. It fails to recognize that the economy is merely one aspect of a whole ecological and social fabric. The basic error of the social sciences is to divide this fabric into fragments, assumed to be independent and to be dealt with in separate academic departments – psychology, economics, political science, etc.

Economists neglect social and ecological interdependence, treating all goods equally, without consideration of the many ways in which they are related to the rest of the world, and reducing all values to that of private profit-making. Conventional economics is thus inherently anti-ecological. It uses its concepts – efficiency, productivity, profit, etc – without their wider social and ecological context, and generally neglects the social and environmental costs generated by economic activity.

Such an attitude is not only in sharp contrast to that of traditional cultures, but is also inconsistent with the views of modern physics. The basic theories of modern physics, as I shall show below, force us to see the natural world as an organic whole in which all parts are interdependent; a dynamic system which is self-balancing and self-adjusting, unlike our current economy and technology which recognize no self-limiting principle. The faith in undifferentiated economic and technological growth has become central to our culture. Our economic system is based on continuing expansion, but unlimited expansion on a finite Earth can never lead to a state of dynamic balance. As Schumacher said: 'In the subtle system of nature, our technology acts like a foreign body, and there are now numerous signs of rejection.'

What we need, then, is a new philosophical basis for economics and technology, a new underlying world-view. Such a world-view, I believe, is provided by modern physics, the science on which technology is based.

Quantum Theory

The exploration of the atomic and subatomic world in

the twentieth century has revealed unsuspected limitations of classical concepts and has forced us to revise many of our basic ideas about reality. One of the main insights of quantum theory, the theoretical foundation of atomic physics, has been the recognition that probability is a fundamental feature of the atomic reality which governs all processes, and even the existence of matter. Subatomic particles do not exist with certainty at definite places, but rather show 'tendencies to exist'. At the atomic level, the solid material objects of classical physics dissolve into patterns of probabilities.

These patterns, furthermore, do not represent probabilities of things, but rather probabilities of interconnections. A careful analysis of the process of observation in atomic physics shows that the subatomic particles have no meaning as isolated entities, but can only be understood as interconnections between the preparation of an experiment and the subsequent measurement. Subatomic particles are not 'things' but interconnections between things, and these 'things' are interconnections between other things, and so on.

Quantum theory thus reveals a basic oneness of the universe. It shows that we cannot divide the world into independently existing small units. As we penetrate into matter, nature does not show us any isolated basic building blocks, but rather appears as a complicated web of relations between the various parts of a unified whole.

Another important insight of atomic physics has been the realization that this cosmic web of relations includes the human observer and his or her consciousness in an essential way. In quantum theory, the observed 'objects' can only be understood in terms of the interaction between various processes of observation and measurement, and the end of this chain of processes lies always in the consciousness of the human observer.

The crucial feature of quantum theory is that the human observer is not only necessary to observe the properties of an atomic phenomenon, but is necessary even to bring about these properties. My conscious decision about how to observe, say, an electron will determine the electron's properties to some extent. In other words, the electron does not *have* objective properties independent of my mind. In atomic physics, the sharp Cartesian split between mind and matter, between the I and the world, is no longer valid. We can never speak about nature without, at the same time, speaking about ourselves.

Relativity Theory

The changes in our basic concepts of reality discussed so far have all been brought about by quantum theory, one of the two basic theories of modern physics. The other theory, which has influenced our conception of nature just as deeply, is Einstein's theory of relativity.

Relativity theory has brought about a drastic change in our concepts of space and time. It has shown us that space is not three-dimensional and that time is not a separate entity. Both are intimately and inseparably connected and form a four-dimensional continuum called space-time. In relativity theory, therefore, we can never talk about space without talking about time and vice versa.

The concepts of space and time are so basic to the description of natural phenomena that their modification entails a modification of the whole framework we use to describe nature. The most important consequence of this modification is the realization that mass is nothing but a form of energy; that even an object at rest has energy stored in its mass.

These developments – the unification of space and time and the equivalence of mass and energy – have had a profound influence on our picture of matter and have forced us to modify our concept of a particle in an essential way. In modern physics, mass is no longer associated with a material substance, and hence particles are not seen as consisting of any basic 'stuff', but rather as bundles of energy. Energy, however, is associated with activity, with processes, and this implies that the nature of subatomic particles is intrinsically dynamic.

To understand this better, it must be remembered that these particles can only be described in a framework where space and time are fused into a four-dimensional continuum. In such a framework, the particles can no longer be pictured as static three-dimensional objects, like billiard balls or grains of sand, but must be conceived as four-dimensional entities in space-time. Subatomic particles are dynamic patterns which have a space aspect and a time aspect. Their space aspect makes them appear as objects with a certain mass, their time aspect as processes involving the equivalent energy. Relativity theory thus gives the constituents of matter an intrinsically dynamic aspect. The being of matter and its activity cannot be separated; they are but different aspects of the same space-time reality.

The energy patterns of the subatomic world form the stable atomic and molecular structures which build up matter and give it its macroscopic solid appearance, thus making us believe that it is made of some material substance. At the macroscopic level, this notion of substance is quite useful, but at the atomic level it no longer makes sense. Atoms consist of particles and these particles are not made of any material stuff. When we observe them, we never see any substance;

what we observe are dynamic patterns continually changing into one another – a continuous dance of energy.

Implications for Science and Society

What, then, are the implications of the New Physics for science and for society? One of the main lessons that physicists have had to learn in this century has been that all the concepts and theories we use to describe nature are limited. Whenever we expand the realm of our experience, we have to modify, or even abandon, some of these concepts. The experience of questioning the very basis of one's conceptual framework and to be forced to accept profound modifications of one's most cherished ideas has been dramatic and often painful for physicists, especially during the first three decades of the century, but it was rewarded by deep insights into the nature of matter and the human mind. I believe that this experience may be very useful for other scientists, many of whom have now reached the limits of the classical Newtonian world-view in their fields. To transcend the classical models, they will have to go beyond the mechanistic and reductionist approach, as we have done in physics, and develop holistic and ecological views.

Thus, physicians will have to widen their perspective, shifting their focus from disease to health, seeing the human organism as a dynamic system which shows interrelated physical and psychological aspects, and relating the general condition of this system to its physical, emotional and social environment.

Similarly, psychologists will have to expand the framework of classical psychology to gain a deeper understanding of the human psyche. Like physicians, they will have to deal with the whole organism, seeing it as a dynamic system which involves interdependent physical and psychological patterns; a system which is an integral part of interacting larger systems of physical, social, cultural and cosmic dimensions.

The social sciences will have to deal with these larger systems accordingly, transcending present disciplinary boundaries and expanding their basic concepts from their narrow, reductionist connotations to a broad social and ecological context. This will be the only hope for modelling and managing our present economic and social institutions which have developed to a point where they have become a major threat to our well-being.

In many of these fields, scientists will be able to model their new concepts after those of modern physics. For others, physics may not be appropriate as a model but will still be helpful. Scientists will not need to be reluctant to adopt a holistic framework, as they often are today, for fear of being unscientific. Modern physics will have shown them that such a framework would be not only scientific; it would be consistent with the most advanced scientific theories of physical reality.

For the further development of science, the general recognition that all scientific theories have to be limited and approximate will be of crucial importance. The science of the future may well consist of a network of interlocking theoretical models, none of them being any more fundamental than the others. Such an approach seems to be best suited to describe the multi-levelled, interrelated fabric of reality. The various models, ultimately, will go beyond disciplinary distinctions, using whatever language will be appropriate to describe different aspects and levels of reality.

The fundamental cultural significance of such a development would be the recognition that all rational

135

approaches to reality are limited. Broad acceptance of this fact will be a necessary step towards a more balanced culture. In such a culture, science as a whole would be only one of many ways pursued by men and women to deepen their understanding of the cosmos. It would be complemented by the intuitive ways of poets, psychics, mystics and many other, equally valid, approaches. Thus, our attitudes and values would become balanced. We would fully realize, as the Chinese sage Chuang Tzu said, that 'life is the blended harmony of the *yin* and *yang*'.

Discussion

*What is the relationship between Matter and
Consciousness?*

The patterns we observe in matter seem to be reflections of patterns of mind. When you observe a certain
particle or certain structures in the particle world it is
very difficult to say whether it is actually out there or
whether it is in the mind. It seems to me that patterns
of mind and patterns of matter are reflections of one
another. When we study matter, we end up with interconnections and correlations, and we see that material
structures turn out to be a network of correlations.
When we deal with mind, the psyche, in the realm of
thought, of consciousness, we deal with interconnections and correlations. So we have two sets of correlations, and there are correlations between these two
sets of correlations. I think this is the way that we can
really make contact between matter and consciousness.
As long as matter was seen as a solid object there was
no way we could relate it very well to consciousness,
but now that we see a web or network in the psychological field and in the material field there is a hope of
making some connection.

Fritjof Capra

What effect do these theories have on the consciousness of physicists as people?

One of the differences between physics and mysticism is that mystical knowledge cannot be obtained just by observation but only by changing your whole way of life – by very integral, intimate involvement of your whole being. You could almost say that this existential transformation itself is the knowledge. The knowledge is the transformation. Now, in science this is not true. Most scientists are able to develop these theories with beautiful and profound philosophical implications and then go home and live a very Newtonian life. This is because the intellect can detach itself from reality. However, this does not apply to all scientists by any means, and, typically, the really great ones such as Einstein show the influence of these theories in their lives. The most intuitive physicists show this blending of their lives and their work. But there is a whole army of physicists who can work out the theories without them having a major impact on their lives.

How do you see the Christian view of God?

The image of a creator God who imposes His divine law on the universe is very much in conformity with the classical world-view of fixed natural laws and of the universe working like a machine according to these strictly deterministic laws. This sort of rigid Christian view was not the world-view of mystics. The numerous mystics of the Christian tradition had a very different view of God, and for that very reason they were not really recognized by the hierarchy of the Church. Mystical traditions in the West have been suppressed.

Discussion

Will you comment on medical scientists and doctors, please?

My next book is going to be about health in a very broad context. I shall talk about three dimensions of health: individual health, social health and ecological health. Individual, society and ecosystem. And I shall suggest how to broaden the mechanistic framework which I agree is very strong in medicine. In the United States I can see that there is a strong popular movement, a strong grass-roots movement towards health care and I think that, as in economics and politics, the change will come from people and not from the authorities. This is going to happen in medicine, particularly, because we have a lot of power to bring to bear in the medical field. When I have a sore throat I don't have to take a throat lozenge, knowing that it will kill the bacteria but at the same time weaken the organism, I can turn to other means. By not buying the drug, you do something which is not only healthy for yourself, but which is also healthy socially, economically and ecologically. In other words if you have a headache and you don't take an aspirin, I consider this to be a political act.

Why do you call it New Physics?

The basic point is that we are seeing the universe as a unified cosmic process, and all objects, people and events as patterns in the process. You can't separate any one pattern from the rest without destroying it. This is quite obvious when you are talking about living organisms, such as a bird or a cat – separate that organism from the environment, the air and everything, and you kill it right away. New Physics has shown us that this is true also for inorganic matter: that you can also destroy atoms, particles and molecules, if you are able to take them completely out of their environment. What you can do is to separate patterns from the rest conceptually. We have been very successful in doing that. I can say that this cup of water is a separate object and the microphone is a separate object and Satish Kumar is different from me, we are separate, he is not me and I am not him, and so on.

But New Physics has shown us that it is very difficult to separate things in this way. When we go to smaller and smaller dimensions it becomes increasingly difficult to separate any pattern from the whole. You can still do it approximately, but it becomes more and more difficult. So you must start from an understanding of the universe as a whole and *then* concentrate on individual patterns. If you start with the patterns and say they are separate objects, separate building blocks, then you will never understand the whole. That, I believe, is the kernel of New Physics. So it is not a question of how to put things together, but a question of how to start from the whole first and then concentrate on the individual patterns.

What form will the new biology – genetic engineering and genetic research – take and what role does it have?

Biologists are very successful in molecular biology, in breaking things up into pieces and studying molecular mechanisms. It is true that this method does not allow them to understand any biological process, even the simple processes, in a very complete way. But they

understand bits and pieces, and bits and pieces fasci-
nate them so much that the whole strategy of research
in biology is organized along these reductionist lines.
So if you are a biologist you will only get a grant if you
write your grant proposal in those terms, in that
language. This is a field in which change is hard to
foresee except, perhaps, in medicine, because with
medicine it is quite clear, now, that we are coming to
the end of the productionist paradise and we have to
abandon it or modify it. This, I think, will affect
biology.

*Isn't dividing of things a more convenient way to learn
them?*

It is true that we divide things up for convenience, but
we do not have the deeper world-view in our culture
that tells us it is only for convenience. When you grow
up and go to school, you are taught that things are
made of atoms and that atoms are made of particles.
You are not told that it is all cosmic consciousness
which has material patterns, and that these are inter-
connected and it is all a dance and you can conveniently
split up the dance into different movements.

*How does one study organisms in a realistic way and
study them seriously?*

I think Dr de Bono put it very clearly when he said
that 95 per cent of our thinking can be rational but that
5 per cent has to be lateral. I think you could say,
similarly, that you can study the detailed pattern pro-

vided you never let the whole out of sight, and this will make all the difference. Whatever you are going to say about these patterns or individual organisms or functions is going to be approximate. The notion of models is extremely important. The map is not the territory. It is only an approximate representation of reality. It is a very profound change of attitude, a real revolution.

In teaching science, how could you start from a realistic and not a mechanistic perspective?

I teach courses about modern physics for non-physicists. It would be very interesting to do that even with small children. Start in a poetic way. In the first two classes tell them about this cosmic dance and everything in an unscientific way, a poetic way, and then say to them, 'Now, we are going to look into the details, but remember that you will have to unlearn some of them later, so don't believe them very firmly. It is not 100 per cent true, it is just a model.' I don't know how this can be expressed in language that secondary school children will understand, but I think it is worth doing. It really is something that should be tried out. Something like this is done in the Steiner schools, where they start with myth and with a lot of painting, and then go on to become more intellectual.

In the teaching of science or physics, there is this myth of a scientist sitting at his desk – I say his because it is always a man – and working everything out from the basic equations in a very rational way. Now, when you do science this is not at all how science is done, there is a lot of guesswork, a lot of intuition, a lot of synchronicity, but this is not acknowledged. In our educational system, in the teaching of science, there should be courses about the development of intuition. There are various exercises that you can learn to help develop intuition, although this is only beginning to be recognised.

What is mind?

I don't know. I was very impressed with Gregory Bateson's new book, *Mind and Nature*. He sees mind as a systems property of living organisms and he lists five conditions which have to exist before you can speak of something as having mind, or thinking. This goes far beyond the development of the nervous system on its own. It starts much earlier in living organisms and is a certain way of processing information, using information for survival. I think what it comes down to is that there is a certain complexity of interconnectedness that allows you to speak about mind. You can make the connection to matter by saying that matter also has this interconnectedness and maybe there are similarities or images and so on. So I think that to read Bateson's book is the best I can suggest.

VI
Lateral Thinking

Edward de Bono

When I wrote my first book, *The Use of Lateral Thinking*, I had not yet invented the term 'lateral thinking', so throughout the book I referred to the process as 'the other sort of thinking'. One day I was trying to explain this other sort of thinking to a journalist, and I said that instead of moving straight ahead to tackle a problem you could move laterally in order to change the approach. Having used the word 'lateral' I realized its suitability and have used it ever since. The term 'lateral thinking' is now officially part of the English language, being recognized in the Oxford English Dictionary. In fact, it is even in the pocket version of the dictionary. There is, so I am told, also a British Standard (BS 3138 (1979)).

Why was it necessary to invent the term 'lateral thinking'? If it is to do with the creation of new ideas then why is the term 'creative thinking' not good enough? The two expressions are by no means synonymous, although both may have as an end result new ideas. Let us take the case of a highly creative painter. He sees the world in a way different from the rest of us. His talent for expression and his emotional sensitivity allow him to convey that different view in such a way that we come to see the world through his eyes, through his work. Such an artist is of great value to society because the purpose of art is exactly that enlargement of vision. In figure 1, I have shown the broad

144

stream of common perception and the separate perception of the artist. But though the perception of that artist may be different and most valuable, it may never change. The artist himself may be quite unable to look at the world in a different way. In fact, he may be rather rigidly trapped within his own perception and for the whole of his life may work within that perception. This in no way lessens his value for society – on the contrary, it may hone that perception to make it even more powerful. This rigidity of perception is, however, quite the opposite of lateral thinking. The lateral thinker is able to change the way he looks at things. The possession of a different way of looking at things may be an example of lateral thought but does not necessarily indicate a lateral thinker.

I work a lot with young children and I am always amazed by their freshness of approach and originality. If they are presented with a problem they will usually come up with a novel approach quite different from what a adult might offer. The result may be a brilliant example of lateral thought, but the children are not necessarily lateral thinkers. A child does not know the

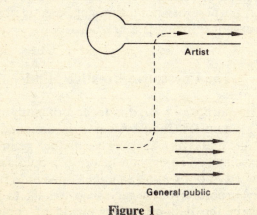

Figure 1

established approach to a problem, so he creates his own individual, and often original, approach. But if he is then asked to come up with a different approach he may be unable and even unwilling to try. In short, the child has an original way of looking at the problem but may be rigidly trapped within that original way. So both the artist and the child may be highly creative but neither may be a lateral thinker. I am conscious that I have made this distinction rather sharply in order to illustrate why the term 'lateral thinking' needed inventing if we were to pay proper attention to this type of thought. In fairness, it should be said that many artists and many children are also lateral thinkers in addition to being merely creative. There are also excellent lateral thinkers who do not possess artistic skills. Lateral thinking is the process of generating alternative concepts and perceptions.

For those who use the traditional psychological jargon of 'divergent' and 'convergent' thinking, it should be noted that lateral thinking is at times divergent and at other times convergent – so it cuts across this classification. If, however, we focus only on the end-product then I do not mind in the least if we agree that the common purpose of lateral thinking, creative thinking and divergent thinking is a new idea.

The Uncreative Creative Mind

The main purpose of mind is to be brilliantly uncreative. As an information system it is designed to be uncreative: that is its main purpose and the main source of its excellence. To explain this rather bold assertion I shall need to bring in a game that I invented recently – for a purpose. I often get asked to talk to people working in the data-processing world of computers.

Computers are so immensely powerful that these people start to believe that there is no such thing as an idea. They come to believe that all you need to do is to measure all the available facts and put them into the computer. The computer is then programmed to put these facts together in every possible combination and to choose the combination that best suits the user's purpose. So I invented the game to illustrate – not prove – that this sort of behaviour was rather unlikely.

The game is a jigsaw consisting of just sixteen small squares that have to be put together to give a large square (four by four). Yet it is so designed that if a person positioned one piece every second day and night, it would take about one thousand million years to be sure of getting it right. Since termites have only been on Earth for one hundred million years and man, at most, for ten million years, that is rather a long time to solve a very simple game. The explanation lies in the fact that the jigsaw is so designed that the player can only tell he has got it right after he has placed the very last piece. There is no simple way of judging which piece to use at any particular moment. So he has to try all possible combinations.

If the human mind worked in this way (trying all possible combinations of the sense data reaching it), it would take us about a month just to cross the road. The brilliance of the human mind lies in its ability to take in a mass of data and to put it together to give a pattern. Once the pattern is established then the mind uses that pattern on all future occasions and so can make quick decisions – and live in the complex world. So the purpose of mind is to establish patterns and then to use them thereafter. So the mind is designed to abolish the need for it to be creative on each occasion. Of course, we could say that the mind was very creative to establish the pattern in the first place, and that is why I called it the uncreative 'creative' mind. As we shall see later, there is a type of information system that automatically creates patterns.

The Mind and Perception

It has always seemed to me that in our treatment of thinking we pay far too little attention to perception. We concentrate rather on the processing of our perceptions. I believe that the most important part of thinking takes place in our perceptions, in the way we look at things. If we get this right then the processing that has to be done is relatively simple. If we get it wrong then no matter how excellent our processing is, we are likely to end up with a daft answer. We have not paid too much attention to perception for a number of reasons. We often assume that there is a standard, accepted way of looking at the world and that all reasonable people would share this common starting-point. We sometimes assume that perception does not really matter and that if the processing part of our thinking is good enough we shall get the right answer. There is even a notion that the strict application of processing will itself determine how the situation ought to have been looked at in the first place. Paradoxically, these fallacies have been shown up by the development of the computer with its superb processing ability. What this has done is to show that no matter how brilliant the processing may be, it cannot make up for inadequate perception – nor can it bring about a better perception. All our processing is done from a chosen starting-point of perception and within a chosen framework of perception. The two main reasons why we have not done more about perception seem to be the following. Most of the thinking traditions that dominate our universities and, indeed, our culture were developed by the scholastic philosophers of the Middle Ages who had to use their thinking to prove wrong the various heretics who attacked the established faith. Since it is possible in a constructed theology to assume, or establish, common perceptions, there was a proper emphasis on process – usually semantic arguments. The other reason is that perception seems nebulous and intangible compared to the nice formality of processing in mathematics and elsewhere.

I often use a number of illustrations to show the difference between perception and processing. I shall content myself with my favourite. Imagine you are about to make a French salad-dressing and have two glasses standing side by side. One is three-quarters full of olive oil and the other is three-quarters full of vinegar. You now take a tablespoonful of oil from the oil glass and stir it into the vinegar glass. You then take a spoonful of the mixture out of the vinegar glass and return it to the oil glass. At the end of this simple transaction which glass is the more contaminated? Is there more oil in the vinegar glass than vinegar in the oil glass, or what? I posed this problem in my first book and received lots of irate replies from people who had convinced themselves, quite logically, that I was wrong when I claimed that at the end the amount of oil in the vinegar glass equalled the amount of vinegar in the oil glass. The argument ran as follows. The first spoonful is of pure oil. The second spoonful contains a *mixture* of oil and vinegar. It is obvious that there must be more oil in the pure spoonful than vinegar in the mixture spoonful – so it follows that my claim for equality must be nonsense. The logic is impeccable – but there is an error in perception that I shall try to illustrate in figure 2.

In figure 2 we see one spoonful travelling in one

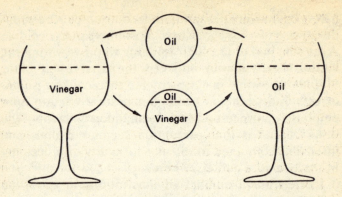

Figure 2

direction and an equal spoonful travelling back in the opposite direction. The first spoonful contains pure oil. The returning spoonful contains a mixture of oil and vinegar. In our minds we can let the two liquids separate – as shown in the figure. Where has the oil in this 'mixture' spoonful come from? In the first place from the mixture glass, but since that contained no oil at the start this oil must have been brought across in the first spoonful. So this little bit of oil has done a round trip and ended up where it started from. So we can forget about it and subtract it from each spoonful. The result is obvious: what is exchanged is equal. The error of perception lay in not taking into account the 'round trip' of some of the oil. To my mind, this is a classic illustration because a small change in perception makes the answer obvious. And, in fact, arithmetic or algebraic solution of this problem is surprisingly tedious.

Although the spoonful of oil and vinegar mixture would actually separate, it is the separation in our minds that matters more. This gives rise to a 'thought experiment' and, as we shall see later, thought experiments are the basis of lateral thinking. Einstein placed a very high value on them and we know how his famous theories arose from just such experiments.

Among my other activities I run what I believe is the largest programme in the world for the direct teaching of thinking as a subject in schools (see *Teaching Thinking*, published by Penguin Books). There are now about five thousand schools using the material, both in the United Kingdom and overseas. One of the main projects of the new Venezuelan Minister for the Development of Human Intelligence is the introduction of this programme into schools in Venezuela. I mention this programme because, although it is distinct from lateral thinking, the whole emphasis is on the perceptual part of thinking rather than the processing.

Perception and Patterns

I often get asked to explain lateral thinking in a few sentences. It simply cannot be done. Suppose I were to say that lateral thinking was the logic of a patterning system? Technically that would be correct, but unless the listener knew all about patterning systems my remark would mean nothing. So I would have to say that it was to do with finding new ideas and new ways of looking at things. The listener would then wonder aloud, and in writing, what was so novel about that, since many people have dealt with the importance of new ideas and new ways of looking at things. That is why I welcome the chance of explaining, at some length, the background to lateral thinking.

Those who would like a fuller description of the nature of self-organizing patterning systems should read my book *The Mechanism of Mind* (published by Penguin Books). What I am going to write here is very brief and superficial.

Let us contrast two types of information receiving systems: the towel model and the gelatine model.

We lay a small bath-towel on a table and place a bowl of ink alongside. We then take a spoonful of ink and empty this onto the towel. An ink-stain results. The ink represents the incoming information and the towel represents the memory system which is affected by this information. The ink-stain is the record or data storage. We place a few more ink-stains and end up with something like figure 3. The towel now carries a good record of the arriving ink-stains. If we wanted to use this stored information we would need an outside 'processor' to read off the information and to use it according to some programme. The result is very like a classic computer with information storage and information processing. It is also like the traditional view of the human mind with 'memory' and 'thinking'.

In our second model we do not have a towel as the memory system. Instead we have a shallow dish of gelatine which has set. We also heat up the bowl of

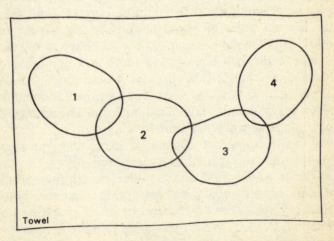

Figure 3

ink. A spoonful of hot ink is placed on the gelatine which then dissolves, but stops dissolving when the ink has cooled down a bit. We then pour off the cooled ink and the melted gelatine and are left with a depression which corresponds to the ink-stain in the towel model – as our mark on the surface. We repeat the same placing and the same sequence of spoonfuls as in the towel model. But we get a very different result: as shown in figure 4. What has happened is that if the second arriving spoonful of hot ink falls anywhere near the depression caused by the first spoonful, then the second lot of ink will flow into that depression and make it deeper, leaving only a shallow depression at the point of arrival. And so it goes on with the third and fourth spoonfuls until a channel is eroded in the gelatine surface. In short, the gelatine surface has provided an opportunity – or environment – in which the incoming information can organize itself into a pattern.

The definition of a pattern is very simple: if one state changes to a particular subsequent state with a greater

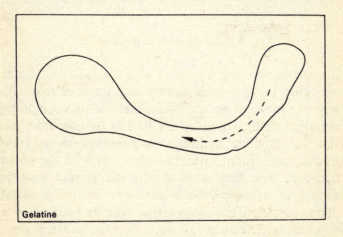

Gelatine

Figure 4

probability than chance, there is a pattern. In the gelatine model, ink placed at one end of the channel will flow to the other end with a probability greater than chance, so there is a pattern. In a patterning system there is no need for an outside processor because there is flow from one part of a record to another. By building up different layers of pattern we can achieve any information processing we like.

It should be noted that the pattern formed in the gelatine model depends on the sequence in which the different spoonfuls of ink arrived. A different sequence would give a different pattern – or none at all.

Those who wonder how this simple gelatine model can relate to information handling in a nerve network should read the book mentioned earlier.

All I have wanted to do here is to show the difference between the usual 'discrete' type of information storage system and the 'patterning' type which provides an environment in which incoming information organizes itself into patterns.

Patterns and Humour

Instead of showing a pattern as a succession of states we could show it more simply as a track or road. At any one moment we are more likely to proceed along the road than to wander off it. Let us now take the simplest possible variation. Suppose there are two tracks, one leading off the other. This is shown in figure 5. You may wonder why the second track is shown as being so much narrower at the point of departure from the main track. This is because in a dynamic system (such as is described in *The Mechanism of Mind*) there can never be two equal tracks. The one which is slightly better established than the other will, for that moment, completely dominate the other.

The implications of figure 5 are rather profound. That is why I chose it as the 'biodic' symbol (from *hodos*, the Greek for road) in my book *The Happiness Purpose* (published by Penguin Books). Figure 5 illustrates the asymmetry of a patterning system. If you start at A you will get to B. But if you start at C you will get to A. In other words the route from A to C is invisible if you start at A but very obvious if you start at C. There is, in effect, an 'information valve'.

It has always surprised me that traditional philosophers have paid so little attention to humour. I write this because, to my mind, humour is easily the most significant characteristic of the human brain. In information-handling terms 'reason' is relatively easy to achieve – just run a sorting system backwards. But humour can only occur in a patterning system. That is why it would be very sinister and very dangerous if computers developed a sense of humour.

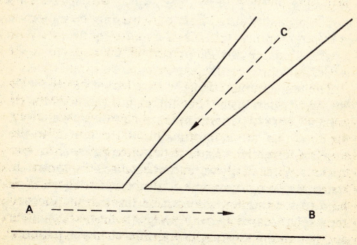

Figure 5

With humour there are essentially two mechanisms, both of which arise from figure 5. The first is the pun mechanism in which the listener is expected to move smoothly from A to B. Then the humorist shows how the double meaning of the word could also have taken the listener to C. In the second mechanism the listener goes from A to B and then the humourist gives the punch line which shows – in hindsight only – how C actually links up with A.

Humour and Lateral Thinking

The mechanism of humour, hindsight, insight and lateral thinking is the same. All four phenomena arise from the asymmetry of patterns. The only difference lies in the end result. With humour we accept C as plausible – for the sake of the joke. With hindsight we accept a logical position which we regard as quite obvious – after we have got there. With insight there is a sudden switch over to a new way of looking at things which probably arises from our entering the pattern at a different point (see *The Mechanism of Mind*). With lateral thinking we adopt certain methods to make easier for ourselves the sideways move from B to C.

The human brain, being so excellent at pattern-making and pattern-using, has rather few methods for escaping from old patterns to reach new ones. We always suppose that more information will cause us to see things differently. This does not often happen, for two reasons. First of all we only look for the information that the old patterns tell us to look for. Second, we tend to see the new information through the old pattern. That leaves us with accident, mistake, humour and lateral thinking as our tools for changing patterns. The history of science shows how effective accident and mistake have been in setting off new ideas (for example, the invention of the triode valve or Pasteur's development of inoculation). Thinkers have not yet learned to take humour seriously. That leaves lateral thinking as the deliberate methodology for changing patterns.

Lateral Thinking as Attitude

We can look at lateral thinking both as attitude and also as process. I was giving a seminar on lateral thinking to a group of very senior Nigerian Civil Servants. At the end of the morning one of them remarked to the course organizer that it was the first time in his life that anyone had given him a logical reason for listening to a subordinate. Until that morning the Civil Servant had felt that he had the knowledge and experience and could call for the expertise, so there was no need to listen to a subordinate. He now saw that looking harder in one direction would not enable him to see in another direction – so his subordinate was worth listening to because he might have a different way of looking at things.

The biodic symbol (figure 5) expresses this attitude. The attitude encompasses the notion that the mind creates patterns of perception according to its sequence of experience (either personally or culturally) and that there might well be another way of looking at things. This is not to say that we treat everything as illusion in the Buddhist or Hindu style. On the contrary, we develop the notion of 'proto-truth' which is described in *The Happiness Purpose*. Instead of the Western adherence to absolute truths as a foundation for belief and behaviour; instead of the Eastern emphasis on the escape from illusion, there is an acknowledgement that we can treat a truth as absolute but at the same time be ready to change it.

So the lateral thinking attitude treats concepts and perceptions as real but temporary organizations of experience which can be changed. There is, therefore, a continual effort to find other ways of looking at things.

Lateral Thinking as Process

In the course of my lectures and writing I often make use of the wheelbarrow illustrated in figure 6 (many other people have borrowed it – usually without permission). I ask the audience to jot down any five comments on the design. When I collect the results there are usually about twenty times as many 'negative' comments as 'interested' comments. It is said to be unstable. The wheel is in the wrong place. The wheel strut is weak. It is more difficult to push down than to lift – and so on. With children the ratio is only about two to one. This is partly because they do not yet know enough about centres of gravity and leverage, and partly because they feel that it is the best wheelbarrow I can draw and they want to be kind to me. From this more positive attitude come a string of suggestions: it would be easier to turn sharp corners; when filling ditches or holes the body of the barrow could move out over the hole and a flap in the bottom dump the load; you could not strain your back, and so on.

Quite naturally – and quite correctly – the adult audiences tend to use 'judgement' as their first operation of perception. Does this design 'fit' what I know about wheelbarrows? Does it 'fit' what I know about levers? Judgement is the most important tool in a pattern-using system. We need judgement in order to identify the pattern (recognition, etc.), and then we

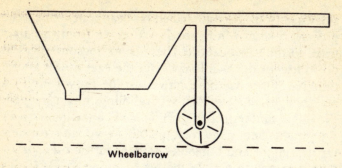

Wheelbarrow

Figure 6

need judgement to make sure that we do not wander off the established track of the pattern.

But if we are using lateral thinking we want to do the opposite. We want to move away from the main track in order to increase our chances of hitting another track, as shown in figure 6. So just as judgement is the basic tool of ordinary perception, so 'movement' is the basic tool of lateral thinking. For the judgement system we have the basic operating tool of the negative, 'no' and its derivatives. In my writing (for example in *Lateral Thinking*) I have tried to introduce the new word 'po' as the operating tool of lateral thinking. 'Po' symbolizes provocation.

Provocation and Stepping Stones

Provocation is one of the fundamental principles of lateral thinking. Provocation is best summed up in the sentence: 'There may not be a reason for saying something until *after* it has been said.' This is quite contrary to normal reason, where there is supposed to be a reason for saying something *before* it is said.

The purpose of provocation is to help us to move

sideways from the established track to a new one. The process is shown in figure 7. We move from the main track to the provocation. There is no 'reason' for us to do so except our will to do so in the exercise of lateral thinking. Once we have moved to the provocation (in our thought-experiment), several things might happen. We might find ourselves drifting back to the main track. We might find ourselves unable to go any further. Or, we might find ourselves so near to the other track that it is now a simple matter to move to C. If this happens, then once we are at C we can see, in hindsight, that this new position makes sense. We can forget all about the provocation that helped us to get there. In this way the provocation acts as a 'stepping-stone'. We use 'po' simply to illustrate that we are offering a provocation.

Many years ago, while discussing river pollution from factories, I offered the provocation: 'po the factory should be downstream of itself.' At first sight that seems a stupid idea but, very quickly, there arises from it the

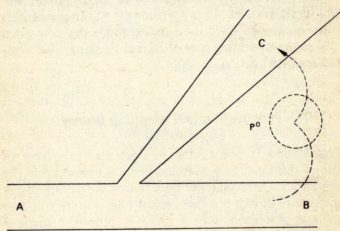

Figure 7

perfectly sensible notion that there should be legislation to ensure that a factory input is always *downstream* of its own output – so the factory is the first to get a sample of its own pollution. That has since become standard legislation in Russia and many East European countries.

On another occasion, when discussing the design of motor-car tyres, the provocation offered was: 'po the wheels should be square.' A large number of interesting ideas arose from this, including the following one. Someone noted that a square wheel would offer great advantages for braking or acceleration because the adhesion area would be so much larger. But it would not roll. So the problem became one of retaining the adhesion advantage and getting rid of the 'no-rolling' disadvantage. The end result was a two-chamber tyre. The inner chamber was at normal inflated pressure, but the outer chamber was at a very low pressure – thus giving a large contact area with the road. So the tyre 'rolled' on the inner chamber and 'adhered' on the outer chamber.

There is much more to lateral thinking than the use of stepping-stones as provocations. There are also many other practical techniques such as concept challenge and random stimulation (see *Lateral Thinking* or *Beyond Yes and No*). What I have tried to do is to illustrate the nature of provocation, because there are various misconceptions about it. Some believe that a provocation is an end in itself: for example, one takes an established concept and then distorts it and leaves it at that. That is rather a simple form of creativity which does not succeed unless the provocation itself becomes a new concept. There is also the notion that provocation in itself is a mission and that it is up to the provoked person (or society) to use the provocation to arrive at a new concept. To my mind, this places too much hope in the ability of society to respond creatively. My view is that provocation is not an end in itself, but a step to a better idea or perception, and that value resides in that. I also feel that the person using the provocation should react creatively to it.

The Application of Lateral Thinking

Lateral thinking can be applied to any concept or perception. The way we look at the world determines the way we deal with it and react to it. The way we look at the world is made up of many concepts and many perceptions (the difference between a concept and a perception is that the former is an organization of ideas and the latter an organization of sensory events – in practice there is much overlap). We can apply lateral thinking to any of them. We can apply it to the concepts of money, earning, capital, industry, economics, education, teaching, productivity or anything else. Nothing is sacred. But the application of lateral thinking is quite different from the application of dialectic attack. Lateral thinking seeks to change and improve through an insight or creative switching rather than through criticism and attack. At a lower level, lateral thinking can be used in problem solving; in opportunity development; in seeking further alternatives for action and decision; in the review and improvement of present activities; in design, and in future scenario construction. Since 'the way we look at things' pervades all thinking, so lateral thinking can be of use at many points.

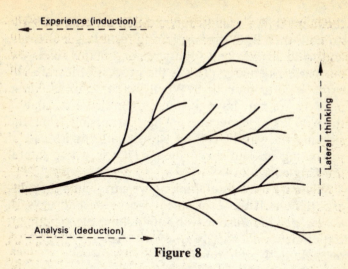

Figure 8

The Place of Lateral Thinking

Just as there are many golf-clubs in the bag and just as we choose the most appropriate one for the circumstances, so are there many types of thinking. Lateral thinking is one of them and we need to use it when it is appropriate. This does not mean that we have no further use for logic or other types of thinking. All have their part to play. But it does mean that we have to temper the usual arrogance of logic with the realization that perception is a very important part of thinking. Perception is to do with the patterning behaviour of mind. And lateral thinking is to do with changing patterns. Lateral thinking is not a luxury. If the mind is a pattern-using system – and all the evidence is that it is – then lateral thinking is a necessity if we are not to be trapped for too long within old patterns of perception.

Figure 8 illustrates the relationship of lateral thinking to the traditional modes of thought. If we imagine that the mind is like a landscape and that experience is like rainfall, then little streams join to form larger streams, and so to rivulets and tributaries and major rivers. So our patterns enlarge. This is the process of learning by experience or induction. When we come to use these patterns we may have to break them down or analyse them. This is deduction. What is missing from the system is a way of cutting across patterns instead of just going up and down them. That is where lateral thinking comes in.

When we use lateral thinking we carry out a thought-experiment. If the experiment works we end up with a new and interesting way of looking at something. Experiments do not always work. But we need to go on making them in our minds.

Appendix I
Coming of the Solar Age

Hazel Henderson

The Six Historic Transitions

I perceive mature Western industrial societies undergoing a profound transition; actually a confluence of at least six historic transitions of differing periodicities:

1. The transition from the Petroleum Age to the now emerging Solar Age, a very rapid cycle most of which is confined to this century.

2. The transition from the Fossil Fuel Age (coal, gas and oil) which began in the early eighteenth century in England, will peak sometime around 2100 and be exhausted around 2300, according to geologist M. King Hubbert's estimates.

This transition from societies living on the earth's stored fossil fuel 'capital' to those living on its daily 'income' (i.e. solar-driven energy, either collected directly for thermal use or converted by solar cells into electricity; or energy stored in falling water, ocean waves, thermal currents and tidal movements, or in the world's climate as wind power) will be an *economic* transition. This is already underway – a move from economies that have maximized material production, mass-consumption and planned obsolescence based on non-renewable resources and energy, to those that minimize waste by recycling, re-using and maintenance based on renewable resources and energy, and which are managed for sustained-yield, long-term productivity.

3.   Thus we also face the transition of *industrialism* itself, as it matures and makes this painful resource-base shift, whether in Britain (where it began), West Europe, North America, Japan (where the process was vastly accelerated) or the Soviet Union, whose younger industrial economy shows signs of 'plateauing' as it also runs into the inexorable energy crunch, and suffers from social bottlenecks in managing complexity that are a characteristic feature of industrialism. And even though in theory socialism is supposed to preclude environmental costs and pollution, in practice, of course, ecological ignorance on the part of commissars and central planning committees can be just as environmentally devastating as that perpetrated by ecologically ignorant corporate executives and their economists.

I have termed this transition stage of mature industrialism as it exhausts its potential as a socio-technical system the 'Entropy State' (in contradistinction to Daniel Bell's linear extrapolation of 'Post-Industrial State' which flourishes from the increasing labour productivity of the agricultural and manufacturing sectors). I define the Entropy State as the stage reached when these societies' complexity and interdependence, their scale and centralization, and the unanticipated side-effects of their technology finally become unmodellable and therefore unmanageable (however many new bureaucracies they create to try to address the proliferating complexity). All of these efforts to co-ordinate anarchistic economic activities and conflicting technological applications; to clean up the mess left by mass production and consumption; to ameliorate social problems and care for drop-outs, addicts, disabled workers and other social casualties; to mediate conflicts and sustain even larger security forces against theft and crime; to keep the air breathable and the water drinkable – all these efforts lead to a burgeoning of social and transaction costs which finally exceed the actual value of production.

In fact, these social costs (for example, the $2.6 billion in claims and the $22 million in clean-up costs for the Love Canal chemical dump in Niagara, New York, and the $60 billion cost to the public of smoking and alcohol addiction) are still *added* to the Gross National Product (GNP), rather than being subtracted. They are probably the only fraction of the GNP that is still growing! Thus these mature industrial societies wind down of their own weight, as does a physical system, into a state of maximum social entropy. Thus they face the basic biological problem of evolution: growth creates structure, then structure inhibits further growth; or, as the dinosaurs' extinction demonstrated 'nothing fails like success'.

Today, mature industrial societies can all be seen drifting towards a soft landing in accidental 'steady states', with inflation masking their declining condition. Indeed, the Morgan Guaranty Bank of New York portrayed the absurdity of the GNP-measured growth efforts by pointing out last year that the US economy has now passed the $2 trillion GNP mark. However, they added that whereas it had taken the country 200 years to reach the first trillion, the second trillion had been added in just seven years, and of that two-thirds had been inflation! Similarly, in my critique of Edward Denison's now famous study for the US Commerce Department (showing that the social costs of pollution control, crime and workplace safety had cost the GNP some $40 billion in the past ten years) I pointed out that we have simply overstated 'growth' and 'productivity' for decades, and now these accrued social bills have to be paid. And in a recent paper by French information theorist Jean Voge, *Information and Information Technologies in Growth and the Economic Crisis* (1977), my concept of the Entropy State is rigorously defined. Voge establishes that the narrow logic of efficiencies in production scale is now meeting diminishing returns, because although production gains are arithmetical they generate information requirements at a geometric rate – thus leading to the familiar explosion of bureaucracy. Voge demonstrates what E. F. Schumacher and I have asserted: that when industrial economies reach a certain limit of centralized, capital-intensive production, they *have to shift direction* to more decentralized economic activities and political configurations, using more laterally-linked information networks and decision-making, if they are to overcome the serious information bottlenecks in excessively hierarchical, bureaucratized institutions. I have referred to this change of direction as a scenario of 'spontaneous devolution', where citizens begin simply to recall the power they once delegated to politicians, administrators and bureaucrats, and the power they delegated to business leaders to make far-reaching technological decisions. The growth in all mature industrial countries of citizen movements for consumer and environmental protection, corporate and government accountability, human rights and social justice; the drive for worker self-management; the growth of the human potential movement and self-help health care; 'small is beautiful' technologies; alternative life-styles and the rise of ethnic pride and indigenous peoples – all these are parts of this 'spontaneous devolution' of old, unsustainable structures.

4. The socio-economic transition will be accompanied by a *conceptual transition* as the 300-year-

old logic underpinning industrialism's rise also reaches exhaustion. The logic stemming from Galileo, Bacon and Descartes, and continuing with Newton, Leibniz and the Enlightenment philosophers: reductionism, materialism, technological determinism and instrumental rationality will fail us. Even the fierce ideological battles of the nineteenth century – which continue today – between capitalism, socialism and communism will re-align, since it is no longer only a question of *who owns* the means of production, but also of the need to address the ecological, social and spiritual dilemmas posed by the *means of production themselves*.

5.   We are also undergoing a *cultural transition*. No one has grasped this cultural transition better than the great sociologist Pitirim A. Sorokin, who in his *Social and Cultural Dynamics* (1937–41) saw this late twentieth-century cultural crisis as the decline of Sensate Culture which has been on the rise since the sixteenth century. Sorokin developed the theory, which he gathered voluminous evidence to support, that human cultures express themselves in three major styles: the *Sensate*, where truth is that which is empirically validated by human senses; the *Ideational*, where truth is revelatory and values are absolute and concern the other-worldly; and the *Idealistic*, those periods where both material and other-worldly concerns and systems of truth and knowledge are balanced and integrated, producing the periods of highest human cultural achievement. Sorokin plotted these three cultural styles in art, music, literature, jurisprudence, technology, systems of knowledge, patterns of war and internal conflict, in dozens of charts covering milleniums from Before Christ to the twentieth century. His description of the decline of Sensate Culture is uncannily predictive of what we see today.

Thus, as Sorokin wrote:

> Western culture is entering the transitional period
> from its Sensate super-system into either a new Idea-
> tional or an Idealistic phase; and since such epoch-
> making transitions have hitherto been periods of the
> tragic, the greatest task of our time evidently con-
> sists, if not in averting tragedy, which is hardly poss-
> ible, then, at least, in making the transition as
> painless as possible. What means and ways can help
> in this task? The most important . . . consists in the
> correction of the fatal mistake of the Sensate phase,
> and in preparation for the inevitable mental and
> moral and socio-cultural revolution of Western
> society.

6.   Yet another approach to today's transition is to
view it as the *decline of systems of patriarchy* that have
predominated in most of the world's nation-states for
some 3,000 years as the earlier matriarchal societies
were superceded. The nation-state, like all patriarchal
systems, is hierarchically structured. It is based on rigid
division of labour, manipulative technology, instru-
mentalist and reductionist philosophies, the control of
information, and on competition, internal as well as
between nations. Unlike the earlier, smaller city-states
and feifdoms, these nation-states have proved – as
Toynbee showed – to be highly unstable, perhaps
somewhat like large, unstable macromolecules. Indeed, nation-states are quintessential expressions of
patriarchal dominance, from the family to the work-
place, community, academia, the Church and all levels
of government. They are characterized by extreme po-
larizations of conceptual, bureaucratic, academic and
intellectual work in centralized, urbanized, metropoli-
tanized complexes. They are rendered operational by
the large statistical aggregates of the formal, monetized

GNP economy. They take no account of the manual tasks, rural life and unpaid work of the non-monetized 'informal economy': household production, gardening, canning, home repairs, nurturing and parenting, volunteer community service and, indeed, all the co-operative activities that permit the over-rewarded competitive activities to be 'successful'.

Today, patriarchal modes are also reaching logical limits: hierarchies become bottlenecks, excessively conceptual government becomes divorced from reality. In Washington, Brussels or Moscow, the bureaucrats try to govern by manipulating statistical illusions, using highly aggregated, averaged data that does not fit a single real situation – while corporate executives make momentous technological and economic decisions using highly selective marketing studies, isolating 'effective demand' from real need as well as from its social and ecological impacts. Similarly, patriarchal academic hierarchies in science and technology have systematically excluded women, denied them patents, admission to professional societies and access to journals. Thus I am operating on the premise that we are, indeed, at a very significant turning-point in human affairs. Only a drastic re-thinking of our entire situation will adequately address our need. It is to this emerging politics of reconceptualization that I have committed myself. Personal responsibility is thrust upon us in such crisis, because external cultural reference-points become lost.

Many cannot bear the burden of living during a period of cultural collapse. As individuals in mass consumption cultures we are used to simple yardsticks of money-measured 'progress' and personal 'success'. The chief taboo of our industrial culture has been the fundamental exploration of questions of human purpose, meaning and identity, and, indeed, of our own finiteness and death. It is painful for all of us, since we can no longer shirk responsibility for the resource-allocation patterns and justness of our society by deferring to the rationalizations of the Enlightenment and Industrial Ages: Lockean individualism, private property (the Latin root *privare* reminds us that originally private property meant that which was denied to the group), technological determinism and 'free market' economics. In other words, we can no longer continue legislating markets and rationing price, and then blaming God for the outcome (the Invisible Hand which Adam Smith found so convenient).

Today, greed has been institutionalized: the economic system is greedy on our behalf, or as Bayard Rustin put it, 'We have socialism for the rich and rugged individualism for the poor.' In fact, we now have an economic system that encourages many of the Seven Deadly Sins – greed especially, pride, sloth (i.e. labour-saving technology) and lust – and whose major logic is based on competition. Our economic system does not even recognize that humans are *also* co-operative and nurturing, enjoy giving as well as getting and are capable of transcending self in the millions of routine volunteer activities and daily acts of altruism. Unfortunately, most mass media also operate under narrow, profit-dominated rules. They believe that reporting 'good news' is less lucrative than the old formula: 'rape, riot and ruin sells newspapers.'

Naturally, my own personal interest in metaphysical reconstruction and in helping to change the world-view and knowledge paradigms of industrial societies necessitates a very long view of such a project. I do not expect to see results in the short run, or even in my lifetime, since these are glacial historic processes. If one is to adopt such an outlandish goal, there are other imperatives. One must change one's own values: a personal self-help project of deprogramming oneself of many of the goals and values our culture promotes – income maximization, institutional careerist goals, material consumption as an end in itself or for display, conventional ego-rewards and competitive individualism. Of course, some of these are deeply instinctive motivating forces, and need to be sublimated in more useful, appropriate ways than those portrayed in the incessant media bombardment of advertising.

One must not only construct a personal life-style that allows one to pursue one's concerns. One must also, in an interdependent society, find relevant means of political expression and action. What does one do after getting right with oneself, after one has achieved a 'right livelihood', but extend concern to one's community and country and begin to act politically as well? Too many feel that virtue now resides in those who head for the hills, build a passive solar house and relinquish all interest in the evils of politics. We cannot evade the responsibility for the power we allowed to drift up to the national level; it is simply too dangerous to ignore. For me, politics has meant organizing interest groups around issues of corporate accountability, and trying to act as a one-woman truth squad for the economics profession. But one must also sustain oneself physically, and if true to one's life project this may render one unemployable! For me, this has meant being self-employed and keeping income requirements to a minimum. If one is *employed* as a full-time futurist by an institution, however worthy, one soon falls into the habit of viewing the future with the interests of that institution in mind. I believe that, to be able to look at the future from many angles, one must try to put the culture and its institutions at as much of a distance as possible, in order to examine them and write about them without fear.

I believe that, although the dangers are enormous,

the long-term opportunities still exist for the human species to evolve in accordance with its operating principles of co-operation, honesty, peacefulness, sharing and love. However, the next ten years may be a very crucial period, as we have moved rapidly from the Soaring Sixties to the Stagflation Seventies and, now, the Economizing Eighties. Since the shift is not yet widely understood as a basic shift of our resource-base and our entire productive systems to renewable-resource, sustained-yield systems, there is much confusion. Leaders still talk of 'consuming our way back to prosperity' – dosing the economy with tax cuts to stimulate demand while exhorting us to believe that there is an energy crisis. The new edict of 'fighting inflation' is an economic mystification, since what we call 'inflation' is just all the social, psychological and ecological variables that economists leave out of their models coming back to haunt us. I have speculated as to whether there is any such thing as profit which is not won at the expense of an equal but unrecorded debit entry in some social or environmental ledger, or passed on to future generations (for example, the huge uncounted costs of decommissioning nuclear reactors which our children will pay in some twenty years).

Obviously, the huge shift in production systems we must make will cause painful grinding of gears and readjustments. However, renewable-resource economies can provide useful, satisfying work for all citizens, as we adapt to economics on a more personal scale and combine our precious capital and resources with more people in the streamlined enterprises, co-operatives and localized economies of scale that higher transportation costs will necessitate. But such new societies of the Solar Age cannot provide windfall profits, large pay differentials, huge permanent war machines and costly space ventures, nor can they supply us with all the frivolous, unnecessary and downright harmful goods we have come to expect as our birthright. We shall have to make political choices between hundreds of brands of headache- and sleeping-pills, cigarettes, protein hair shampoos for pets and expensively advertised and packaged junk foods, and the need for public spending on decent schools, health care, and maintenance of essential services in our cities. When we begin to account accurately for all of the social costs of these frivolous 'goods', we shall soon realize that not only can we not afford them, but that we do not want them. As long as advertisers are allowed to promote only the 'good news' about these products and do not have to tell truthfully of the 'bad news' of the social and environmental effects, individuals will not be able to make informed choices, either politically or in the marketplace. If corporations are allowed to continue manipulating media information by portraying our choices narrowly, as between going along with their priorities or being thrown out of work and freezing in the dark, or forcing workers to choose between their jobs and their health, then our debate will remain cloudy and intergroup conflicts will be fomented.

The new challenges to material expectations in all industrial countries will leave many people frustrated and increasingly despairing of our political system. As we see, services for the poor in cities are the target for budget-cutting. In the US we see unconscionable proposals to break faith over social security entitlements earned long ago. Cutting government spending is an empty shibboleth unless it focuses on special interest boondoggling and some of the vast tax subsidies to corporations, military contractors and energy industries, as well as investment tax credits which are just as often used to further automate and destroy jobs as they are to create them. One can expect increased intergroup conflict, violence and political outbursts, such as Proposition 13 in California, and simplistic demands to cut individual taxes and stimulate investment irrespective of *what* is to be produced. Our politicians will need to be realistic and help us to accommodate to lower material expectations. If the GNP pie cannot grow, then we must face the fact that it is now full of inflationary air and additives unfit for human consumption anyway. We should redefine it more realistically, if economists will let us, and then share the newly baked, wholesome pie more fairly. However, there is the last-ditch economists' effort to define our problems in their terms, as 'declining productivity', 'loss of innovation' and 'inflation' – and hence the need to cannibalize the body politic by 'deregulating', and 'reducing government interference' in the 'free market-place', etc. The rationale is used to lower smog standards, reduce worker job-safety, cut children's school-lunch programmes and funds for summer jobs for unemployed young people, because the costs in social disorder, public health and safety are born by the public, not by producers, who wish to continue the time-honoured practice of 'externalizing' them from company budgets. Meanwhile corporate executives continue to make their speeches about private enterprise while lobbying for huge government subsidies and contracts, and military budgets soar.

I believe that decentralists working on pragmatic alternatives in their own lives cannot ignore politics, and must work to prevent and reduce real hardship and speak out against the sick economists' game of trying to wring inflation out of the system by throwing the economy into recession every three years or so. Even honest economists such as the US's Arthur Okun now admit that today 'You get so little deflation out of a recession that it's like burning down your house to bake a loaf of bread.' Yet Western democracies still seem bent on proving Karl Marx's prediction that late-stage capitalism would need an 'industrial reserve army' of hard-core unemployed, as our own poor minorities and female populations must serve as the last hired and first fired in order to stabilize inflation. We also know that the 'old time religion' favoured by Conservatives and monetarists fails to address the basic new sources of inflation. We must now debate openly our *values* and our public policy *goals*, rather than continue the game of throwing specious data and studies at each other, with the pork-barrel prize going to the interest group with the greatest computer fire-power and the largest army of intellectual mercenaries. I hope that all of us will boo off the platform any politician who refuses to be honest about what part of the Budget he or she intends to cut: whether nuclear aircraft carriers or children's school lunches.

David and Elizabeth Dodson-Gray see the coming period of social adjustment and accommodation to new realities as analogous to the processes described by Elizabeth Kübler Ross in individuals dealing with death: first denial, then anger, followed by bargaining, depression and finally acceptance. But we must remember that in all biological systems decline and death is the pre-condition for *rebirth*, and we must propagate the many scenarios of cultural rebirth and point to the visible, growing edges of the emerging counter-economy and renewable-resource technologies as glimpses of the more humane, communal, co-operative civilizations of the coming Solar Age. Polls are now showing that Americans are adjusting their earlier expectations, and the famous Voluntary Simplicity report of the Stanford Research Institute estimates that 4–5 million Americans have already dropped out of the 'rat-race', leading lives of voluntary frugality and searching for inner growth and psychic riches.

And we can see also how such value shifts are translating themselves into public policy. Such public pressure has affected the evolution of official US Government energy-demand forecasts, where since 1972 the forecasts of energy demand have fallen from 160 quadrillion BTUs to 140 in 1974, to 124 in 1976, and to approximately 95 quadrillion BTUs in the recent Domestic Policy Review of the Department of Energy's forecasts in 1978. Thus we slowly move from the technological fix, the instrumental 'supply side' economists' approach to our problems, to a more subtle, self-aware view of the 'demand side' – our own behaviour, attitudes and values.

Similarly, we see many other examples of hierarchies losing their grip of the issues, and their patriarchal remedies – more centralization, more control, manipulation, technical fixes – are becoming less effective and less credible. We now see the absurdity, as E. F. Schumacher pointed out, of societes that *require* a breakthrough a day to keep the crisis at bay! Charismatic, patriarchal leadership styles are also becoming hollow, from the Imperial Presidency to the pathetic spectacle of leaders such as Israel's Prime Minister Begin and Egypt's President Sadat constantly talking of love, babies and grandchildren, without being aware of the deeper truth they are affirming – that competitive, patriarchal nation-states, and all organized systems of distrust and inequality, have exhausted their logic. Patriarchal leadership seems to have little left to offer except competition, violence, confrontation and institutionalized paranoia with ever greater efforts to manipulate nature for short-term goals.

Thus the value shifts will need be fundamental enough not just to redesign our technologies, reconceptualize our politics and repattern our knowledge, but to reinfuse and rebalance our male-dominated industrial culture with those values to which highest lip-service is always paid but which are *most burdensome and challenging to put into practice*. These values have most often been designated as 'female' and have been thrust upon women and subordinated groups in all cultures – co-operation, humility, nurturing, maintenance, openness, spontaneity, peacefulness and love. Not that it is possible or even desirable to return to the ancient matriarchal systems of our past, but a new synthesis that allows individuals to express a healthier balance of these so-called male and female tendencies is now necessary. The Chinese *yin* and *yang* symbolism is a less painful polarization of the debate and may help us avoid yet another battle of the sexes. Our culture simply suffers from an overdose of *yang*.

Indeed, decentralist, simple communities embody those values *yang* cultures have despised as 'feminine'! Yet these 'sissy' *yin* principles imbue religious doctrines, however patriarchal the formal, administrative Church hierarchies. Dr Elaine H. Pagels, in her recent paper, 'What Became of God the Mother?: Conflicting Images of God in Early Christianity', explores the rationalizations in early Christian sects for the subjugation of women within the orthodox Christian Church. Typical of the fruitfulness of today's fundamental questioning of all our institutions and existing rationales, Pagels has unearthed many references to early Christian sects who believed (more correctly, I should think) that God is a dyadic entity. She has also shown that many of the early Jewish and Christian gnostic texts, which abounded in feminine symbolism as applied to God, were attacked and condemned to oblivion as heresies as early as AD 100–150. In addition, many of these early Christian texts referring to a female divinity and an androgynous creator were rejected as hetero-dox, and only a selected list of 26 were approved as orthodox and became incorporated as texts in the New Testament (*Signs*, Univ. of Chicago Press. Winter 1976, vol. 2 no. 2. p. 293). So we need to re-examine these deepest roots of our belief if we are to deal adequately with the confluence of crises we face. For today, our shattered cultures need creative nurturing, they need 'mothering'.

I believe that our decency and goodwill as citizens in the face of all this obfuscation and confusion will be taxed as never before. We must all involve ourselves in the task of behavioural adaptation to more shared, communal life-styles and the ethic of enough, since these will be the new survival-orientated values of adapting to inevitable new realities: holism, ecological awareness, empathy, co-operation to leaven the excessive competition, justice and fair shares for the poor – what Erich Fromm calls the shift *From Having to Being*. Keeping up with the Joneses will need to be replaced by the *Shakertown Pledge*, and by setting examples to reinforce its points. I believe we see today that ancient faiths are confirmed by empirical events: all the greatest spiritual leaders throughout history have been the real futurists – but we did not always understand their time frame. Cyclic value changes are the history of human societies. Wholesale value-shift in human behaviour will continue to occur, since we are now receiving direct feedback and reinforcement from the Creation – the planet itself. Ancient religious concepts become understandable as scientific formulae: the Hindu concept of *karma* is merely a general systems theory statement of the behaviour of a non-linear system where the vectors of human behaviour may be unknown, but what is known is the certainty that all such motions initiated will boomerang and create complex effects in delayed and displaced patterns. Similarly, the Christian and Judaic concept of Judgement Day is in general systems-theory terms simply a complex non-linear system whose information feedback loops are speeding up to real time, where cause and effect are simultaneous and there is no temporal or spatial dimension in which to hide the consequences of one's actions. Even 'miracles' are simply general statements of non-linearity and of the new mutual-causal paradigms now emerging in information theory and post-Newtonian quantum physics. Indeed, we are still communicating in many disciplinary and sectarian tongues: the Tower of Babel haunts us yet. But the core of knowledge and understanding is the same. In a large enough context, as a species of hominids occupying the same wondrous blue planet, all our self-interests are revealed as identical. Morality has at last become pragmatic.

Appendix II
Appropriate Technology

Leopold Kohr

My discussion of Appropriate Technology centres on the general philosophic question: What is appropriate in the scheme of things?

The idea of 'appropriate' implies the existence of limits. When something is inappropriate, it means it is either too large or too small, too advanced or too retarded, too slow or too fast, too rich or too poor. As the prince of advertisers, the late Howard Gossage, used to say when he defined poison as 'too much', so also we can say of the 'inappropriate' that it can be defined quite simply as 'too much' – too much in either direction. It is as inappropriate to be too virtuous as it is to be too depraved.

Like the Greek idea of harmony, of nothing to excess, the concept of 'appropriate' is therefore a relative one. It depends on what it serves. It is measured by its ability, not to reach the pole to which the needle of the compass points, but to stay on course once the direction is set. What matters is not truth but whether truth is bad or good, whether it builds or whether it destroys. When the Lord proclaimed that there were stars, planets, water and earth, he lied the blue out of the sky because nothing of the sort existed before. They became real when he pronounced the Word. And the Word was a Lie. But it was the only thing appropriate for anyone intent on creating something out of nothing.

The concept thus being a relative one and taking its measure from the thing it serves, the first question we must answer is: Appropriate to what? When speaking of technology, the consensus of most is that it refers to high productivity. The greater this is, the more appropriate is the technology required to improve the human lot. This is what caused the underdeveloped world to try to catch up with the industrialization of the developed world, and the developed world to push for ever higher levels of automated efficiency. Neither has as yet fully grasped that there can be such a thing as *over*development; that beyond given limits technological progress not only ceases to be a solution in the struggle for social advance but actually becomes the most intractable obstacle to it; and that overdevelopment can bedevil not only the developed but also the underdeveloped.

This gives rise to a second question. If the concept of 'appropriate' is defined by limits below which there is not enough and above which there is too much, what determines the limits? The answer is not too difficult. They are set by the size and shape of a thing which, in turn, are determined by the function a thing has to perform. The appropriate size of a tooth depends on its function to make food more readily digestible by breaking it up without hurting in the process the mouth in which it is embedded. A larger tooth would not solve the problem of growth but create a more severe problem of form, even though it might now qualify for entry into the *Book of Records*.

Similarly, the human body, the shell of a snail, a home, a shirt, a school, a theatre, a parliament building, an airport, have the limits to their size determined by their functions. As the Cambridge biologist D'Arcy Thompson has shown in his masterful study *On Growth and Form*, if a snail were to add a single ring to the

183

sturdy structure of its shell once it has reached appropriate size, it would increase the latter's volume sixteen-fold with the result that the structure, which was meant to shelter it, would crush it under its functionless overweight – which may be useful for a collector but hardly for the snail.

And what is true in relation to the size of a shell, a tooth, a theatre or the human body is also true when we apply the concept of 'appropriate' to the size of a community, a society or the state, as well as to the technology best suited to assist these organizations in the discharge of the functions for the sake of which we have created them.

This brings us to a third question which must be answered before we can deal with the question of what is an appropriate technology: What is the function of society which given technology is to serve? What are the benefits of a bonded existence within a community which have induced man to sacrifice the freedoms he could have enjoyed by living on his own rather than in company? Is it justice and peace? If that is the function of society, it would have been wiser to stay away rather than join it. Is it the conquest of the moon which the first astronaut has described as a 'dirty beach' (in contrast to the Pope who more poetically saw in it 'the pale lamp of our dreams')? Is it to unite mankind in a Tower of Babel which, though the Lord destroyed it because he considered it a blasphemous violation of His design, has now been set up in its second materialization in the midst of the cocktail bars of Manhattan?

None of these 'benefits' would seem worth the price of giving up our individual sovereignty. If we have nonetheless opted for the restrictions of a life in common, we can have done so for only one reason: to achieve what Aristotle called the *summum bonum*, a spiritually and materially better life than the one we could attain by living in solitude. And it is this that determines the answer to the question of what is an 'appropriate' technology: whether it is most efficient, not in material productivity, but in its ability to provide us with the cultural, political, economic and convivial ingredients that make up the *summum bonum*, the good life.

Here is where the question of size comes into the picture. Whether large or small, the function of every society is to provide the citizen with the *summum bonum*. But not every society can do this in equal measure. For as the snail must carry the burden of the shell, so must the citizen carry on his shoulders the burden of the state if he wants to derive any benefit from it. And since these burdens tend to increase geometrically with every arithmetic increase in the size of the state, it follows that beyond given limits these burdens multiply faster than the intellectual and material resources of man necessary to catch up with them. Up to these limits we can balance the mounting membership costs of growing societies by advancing technology to levels of productivity appropriate for coping with the greater problems of larger societies. But once these limits are passed, the social burdens become so vast under the impact of the blinding effect of increasing scale that more must be diverted from personal to social use than any further technological improvement is able to add in the commodities needed for communal survival. As a result, one after the other of the ingredients of the good life that is available in smaller societies must be curtailed as they become afflicted by cancerous overgrowth.

The first to suffer is the fullness of our cultural life. This is why large populations organized in single states can afford, for example, fewer opera houses than the same number living divided into smaller and less costly communities such as the city states of the Renaissance. Next to suffer is the political security we need to enjoy the *summum bonum*. No one in the large cities of size-plagued America ventures any longer to go out for a stroll at night unless he is a terrorist, dead drunk or the Son of Sam. And even externally social bigness bears no solace to those afflicted by it, as Saint Augustine suggested when he asked the Ancient Romans: 'What glory is there to the vastness of empire – bright and brittle like glass and forever in fear of breaking.'

Third to fall by the wayside is our material prosperity. Instead of raising our living standards, the super-efficient technology of automation – the only one that is appropriate for meeting the voracious communication, transportation, integration and survival requirements of overextended communities – actually pushes them downward, a fact which is often hidden under the cover of seeming superabundance. For what it gives us is not more butter on bread but, as the Common Market has shown, more butter on butter until it becomes a mountain so large that it can no longer either be dismantled or distributed. Its very abundance *creates* a problem instead of *solving* one. And the same is true of most other commodities with which progress has showered us, from medical services to cars, refrigerators, houses and even holidays. They are no longer luxuries but remedial commodities necessary, not to improve life, but merely to help us to cope with the added difficulties of living on too vast a scale. Like the greater supply of aspirin tablets, they no longer measure a rise in our standards of health but an increase in the incidence of headaches which we did not have as long as we lived in less nerve-racking smaller societies.

Let me illustrate the inexorable decline of living standards in overgrown societies in spite of their stupendous technological advance by means of an analogy. I know that scientists have had their doubts about the value of analogies ever since the disputes between the *statistikoi* and the *analogikoi* raged in Ancient Greece. Yet, talking in images often clarifies concepts faster than talking in figures which, after all, as the measurements in beauty contests demonstrate, convey images too.

The analogy I have in mind is that of a skyscraper. As it rises, it becomes more splendid with every floor, but above a given height it becomes at the same time increasingly less profitable, until it is finally deprived of all economic sense when it reaches the 400th floor. For as architects have calculated, at that height the entire structure would have to consist of lifts needed to transport the people who could live in it if the lift space did not deprive the glorious structure of all living space. The only employment this kind of building could offer would be to lift boys.

Finally, the last amenity affected by unlimited social growth is the primary and, indeed, founding amenity for the sake of which man has opted for a life in common rather than in solitude. This is the companionship for which our nature makes us crave and which only society can satisfy. But as with the other ingredients of the good life, of Aristotle's *summum bonum*, even the companionship function of society begins to shrivel when populations start spilling over their organic limits. Bursting instead of strengthening the form containing them, they now transform natural man into *Organization Man*, and the convivial crowd into *The Lonely Crowd*, as the titles of two well-known books suggest.

For all this, as with skyscrapers, the society best

suited to fulfil its function of providing its members in the highest possible degree with the prosperity, security, cultural serenity and conviviality which, in their sum, make up the good life, is not the *largest* possible society as the contemporary Babylonians fancy with their visions of ideological, economic, continental and world states. It is the society that can give us all this with the *smallest* number of people.

This is not the same as the smallest *society*. It means a society of *limited* size, one that takes its measure, not from what the vast potential of technology can achieve, but from what the small stature of man can absorb. In antiquity, city states with populations numbering as few as twenty or thirty thousand people proved large enough to form some of the most satisfying communities that ever existed. Today, improvements in transport and communication technology has made it possible to extend these limits to perhaps twelve or fifteen million. But beyond this, as the shaky position of the contemporary great powers as well as of the size-afflicted underdeveloped world so glaringly demonstrates, no further technological improvement can match the geometrically multiplying problems of scale then setting in, and annihilating anything that up to that point might have been gained by the economies of scale. They now turn into the *Diseconomies of Scale*, to mention with your permission the subtitle of my latest book. For, to quote Aristotle once more, 'there is a limit to the size of states as there is to other things, plants, animals, implements; for none of these retain their natural power when they are too large or too small, but they either wholly lose their nature, or are spoiled.' This is why, in spite of being ringed by the most glittering circle of economists – many of them of Nobel-Prize calibre – the British Government has proved unable to foresee, forestall or prepare for any of the problems besetting it: not strikes, not unemployment, not inflation, not productivity. A handful of street cleaners could have achieved just as much at less cost. It is not for nothing that an increasing number begin to see salvation in *devolution*, the break-up of the United Kingdom into more easily manageable smaller regions, than in the preservation of a unity that makes it burst at its seams.

Having now reached some idea of the function-determined concept of 'appropriate' political *size*, we are at last in a position to turn back to the derivative concept of 'appropriate' *technology*. Once we realize that not only can the highest living standards *also* be attained in smaller communities, but that they can *only* be attained in societies of *limited* size, we can understand why the 'appropriate' technology for providing a people with the *summum bonum* can be very much simpler, cheaper, less advanced and, indeed, less efficient than the one that is necessary for those living in 'skyscraper' economies.

For as the difficulties of living in great multitudes increases geometrically with every arithmetic increase in the size of our social structure, so they also diminish geometrically with every arithmetic reduction of that size. Instead of getting less for more, we now get more for less. Fewer lifts are a sign not of life getting harder, but of our apartments having come closer to the ground. Frequently, all that is needed to improve our living standards without increasing our income is to move from a large to a small community.

When I lived in the galactic expanse of the metropolitan area of San Juan in Puerto Rico, I had to travel sixty miles every day to reach office, home, friends, shops, theatre, recreation facilities and all the other locations in pursuit of an ordinary day's activities. Only an expensive nerve-, space- and fuel-consuming high-technology car enabled me to do this. When I lived in Cambridge, the same activities required a daily spanning of less than three miles which I could handle by means of a pedal-driven low-technology bicycle. And now that I live in Aberystwyth, the distances separating my daily activities have shrunk to less than half a mile which I can negotiate on foot with a vastly superior efficiency than I could ever achieve with a car.

So the answer to the problems of our time lies not in advancing technology to the point where it becomes appropriate to meeting the stupendous survival requirements of a world integrated in monster societies. The answer lies in reducing the monster societies once again to dimensions in which the 'appropriate' tools of human improvement can be furnished by a less advanced, simpler and cheaper 'intermediate' technology.

This does not mean that there is a conflict between the two concepts. It merely means that for smaller societies the *appropriate* technology is an infinitely less costly *intermediate* technology. Considering their reduced maintenance requirements, this is enough – as I have tried to show with the skyscraper analogy – to provide equally high and, indeed, higher living standards than can be achieved in the size-plagued large societies even with the most advanced technology. Moreover, precisely because intermediate technology is *mechanically* less efficient, it is infinitely more efficient in *human* terms since, in this age of scandalous unemployment, it can achieve the highest standard of living only if all hands are employed. Indeed, it is this feature which provides us with the second defining element of the concept of appropriate technology. This is that, besides its ability to offer to every member of society the fullness of the *summum bonum*, it offers to everyone also the dignity of work needed to attain it.

But intermediate technology is not only the appropriate technology for maintaining the high living standards of small countries. It is also the appropriate technology for speeding up the advance of underdeveloped countries where the disemployment effect of superefficient equipment is such that the only area in which the suddenly emerging armies of unemployed can be reabsorbed (lest they turn their energies towards the overthrow of their governments) is the area of either bureaucratic or military service. No wonder that their first sign of progress is often a rise not in welfare, but in power measured by armies of dimensions which in some cases are larger than those with which Alexander conquered the world. Moreover, since no country can afford both industrialization and militarization at the same time, an inappropriately advanced technology leads not only to abject dependence on foreign assistance, but to a commensurate loss of a people's national identity. Only the lower efficiency and expense of an intermediate technology can avert these retarding side-effects of advanced technology. But since intermediate technology cannot produce satisfactory results except on the reduced scale of smaller communities, it can perform its function only if the contemporary underdeveloped large-area states are first dissolved into cantonal systems of highly autonomous development districts.

Only then will small applications of capital produce measurable results. And only then will wealth accumulate not so much because of high productivity, but because of the low cost of maintaining a communal enterprise of moderate size, coupled with reduced dependence on long-distance transport which the nineteenth-century American economist Henry Charles Carey so aptly called 'the heaviest tax on land and labour'. How heavy this has become in a nomadic world that has abandoned self-sufficiency for large-scale economic and political integration can be seen from such preposterous sums as the $200 million which has to be spent by the American airlines alone every year to protect their passengers from a miniscule number of terrorists whose effectiveness is the more devastating the larger the state which they choose as the target of their attack.

Notes on contributors

R. D. LAING was born in Glasgow in 1927, and was educated at Grammar School and at Glasgow University, where he graduated as a Doctor of Medicine in 1951. From 1951 to 1953 he was a psychiatrist in the British Army. He then worked at the Glasgow Royal Mental Hospital in 1955, at the Department of Psychological Medicine at the University of Glasgow in 1956 and at the Tavistock Clinic from 1957–61. He was Director of the Langham Clinic, London, from 1962–5. From 1961 until 1967 he did research into families with the Tavistock Institute of Human Relations, as a Fellow of the Foundations Fund for Research in Psychiatry.

Since 1964, Dr Laing has been Chairman of the Philadelphia Association, 'a charity whose members, associates, students, and friends are concerned to develop appropriate human responses to those of us who are under mental or emotional stress but do not want psychiatric treatment.'

His books include *The Divided Self, Self and Others, The Politics of Experience* and *Bird of Paradise, Knots, The Politics of the Family, The Facts of Life,* and *Do You Love Me?*

AMORY BLOCH LOVINS resigned a Junior Research Fellowship of Merton College, Oxford, in 1971 to become British Representative of Friends of the Earth, a US non-profit conservation group. A consultant physicist (mainly in the US since 1965) he now concentrates on energy and resource strategy. His clients include the OECD, several UN agencies, the International Federation of Institutes for Advanced Study, the MIT Workshop on Alternative Energy Strategies, the Science Council of Canada, Petro-Canada, USERDA, the US Office of Technology Assessment and other organizations in several countries. He is active in international energy affairs, has testified before parliamentary and congressional committees, has broadcast extensively, and has published five books, several monographs, and numerous technical papers, articles and reviews.

IVAN ILLICH was born in 1926. He studied theology and philosophy at the Gregorian University in Rome and obtained a doctorate in history at the University of Salzburg. He went to the United States in 1951, where he served as Assistant Pastor in an Irish–Puerto Rican parish in New York City. From 1956 to 1960 he was Vice-Rector of the Catholic University of Puerto Rico. Illich was a co-founder of the Center for Intercultural Documentation (CIDOC) in Cuernavaca, Mexico, and since 1964 he has directed research seminars on 'Institutional Alternatives in a Technological Society', with special focus on Latin America. Ivan Illich's writings have appeared in the *New York Times,* the *New York Review of Books, Le Monde,* the *Guardian* and *The Times*. He is the author of *Celebration of Awareness, Deschooling Society, Tools for Conviviality, Energy and Equity* and *Medical Nemesis*.

JOHN MICHELL is a dedicated scholar who has spent years researching into and rediscovering the wisdom of ancient civilizations. He caused a sensation when his fascinating and remarkable conclusions became known with the publication of *The View Over Atlantis*, which has subsequently become an international bestseller. He is also the author of *The Flying Saucer Vision, City of Revelation, The Old Stones of Land's End* and *The Sacred Earth*.

His article on 'A Defence of Sacred Measures' (such as the foot, mile and acre), published in *Resurgence* magazine no. 71, has generated a movement for the protection of The Just Measures.

FRITJOF CAPRA took his Ph.D. at the University of Vienna in 1966. Since then, he has been doing research in theoretical high-energy physics at the University of Paris, the University of California in Santa Cruz, Stanford University, and at Imperial College, London. Besides his technical research papers, he has written several articles about the relations between modern physics and Eastern mysticism, and has lectured extensively on this topic to student audiences in England and the University of California in Berkeley. His book *The Tao of Physics* is a world-wide bestseller.

EDWARD DE BONO was born in Malta in 1933, where he attended St Edward's College and then Malta University. He then proceeded as a Rhodes Scholar to Christ Church, Oxford, where he gained an Honours degree in psychology and physiology and then a D. Phil. in medicine. He also holds a Ph.D. from Cambridge. He has held appointments at the universities of Oxford, London, Cambridge and Harvard.

Among his publications are *The Use of Lateral Thinking, The Five-Day Course in Thinking, The Mechanism of Mind, Lateral Thinking, Technology Today, Po: Beyond Yes and No* and *Children Solve Problems*.

HAZELL HENDERSON is an internationally published futurist as well as an activist and the founder of many public interest groups. She is a Co-Director of the Alternative Futures Study Center at Princeton University, and is the author of *Creating Alternative Futures*.

LEOPOLD KOHR is the author of *The Breakdown of Nations, The Overdeveloped Nations, Development Without Aid, The City of Man* and *The Revolt of the Individual*. He is Professor of Political Philosophy at the University of Wales, Aberystwyth.

Schumacher Society

The Schumacher Society was formed following the death of the economist and thinker Dr E. F. Schumacher in 1977, and exists to develop, discuss and use the momentous ideas which he introduced through his writing and speeches.

The Schumacher Society aims to help establish the importance of appropriate scale in technology and in human organization, and to co-ordinate the efforts of individuals and groups searching for ways of living which restore initiative to the individual and contribute to harmony in industrial life. It encourages the preservation of the natural environment as a basis upon which to achieve these aims and, specifically, the use of organic and non-polluting agriculture.

Through meetings, lectures and conferences the Schumacher Society disseminates understanding of and enthusiasm for the vision and ideas of E. F. Schumacher. In particular, its activities include the annual Schumacher Lectures, which are held in the autumn, usually at Bristol University. These lectures bring to audiences contributions from outstanding contemporary thinkers whose ideas have changed our attitudes towards fundamental issues in modern society. Annual Essay Awards have also been established for the best essays on 'people-centred' thinking – that is, how we can create *viable* alternatives to the impersonal and sectarian systems which have been established in our present institutions.

Resurgence magazine is closely associated with the Schumacher Society and provides a major channel for its ideas and events. *Resurgence* promotes new politics and is concerned with small nations, communities, decentralization and ethnic culture – a philosophical, ecological *and* spiritual forum. It is published in Great Britain six times a year, and is available at an annual subscription of £5.

For information about the work and events of the Schumacher Society, or for a subscription to *Resurgence* (cheques should be payable to Schumacher Society), please write to:

The Secretary, Schumacher Society, Ford House, Hartland, Bideford, Devon.

SPONSORS: Maurice Ash; Satish Kumar (Executive Chairman); Gerard Morgan-Grenville; Hazel Henderson; Leopold Kohr; Elaine Morgan; Yehudi Menuhin; Malcolm Muggeridge; Christian Schumacher (President); Edward Goldsmith; Mrs Vreni Schumacher; John Seymour; Ernest Bader.

GOOD WORK

BY E. F. SCHUMACHER

WHAT IS THE PURPOSE OF OUR WORK?

When Dr Schumacher took a look at the plight of businesses today and said 'small is beautiful' he spoke to millions and coined a phrase. In GOOD WORK he addresses a question which is central to most of us and one which is all too often ignored by the economic structure of the Western world. Dr Schumacher maintains that the purpose of man's work is threefold: to produce necessary, useful goods and services; to enable us to use and perfect our gifts and skills and, finally, to serve and collaborate with other people in order to liberate ourselves from inbuilt egocentricity. A job in which one finds no personal satisfaction destroys the soul. With sanity and sensitivity the late E. F. Schumacher offers important and thought-provoking alternatives which point the way to mankind's physical and mental liberation.

'Compulsive reading'
TIME OUT

'The message of this set of essays is beguiling; technology is not the inevitable ruler and real alternatives seem possible'
NEW SCIENTIST

ECONOMICS 0 349 13133 3 £1.95

and don't miss
SMALL IS BEAUTIFUL
A GUIDE FOR THE PERPLEXED
also by E. F. Schumacher in Abacus

THE
CULTURE OF
NARCISSISM

BY CHRISTOPHER LASCH

'Never has the case against narcissism been made with
such an all-embracing sweep'
NEWSWEEK

Freedom from religious superstition has left a gap in our
lives which has been replaced by the creed of self-love,
maintains Christopher Lasch. Emotional shallowness,
fear of intimacy, hypochondria, pseudo-self-insight,
promiscuous pansexuality and dread of old age and death
are the symptoms of the narcissist whose culture has lost
interest in the future. The frantic search for fulfilment –
in the new consciousness movements and therapeutic
culture; in pseudo-confessional autobiographies; in the
replacement of Horatio Alger by the 'Happy Hooker' as
the new symbol of success – is the world of the resigned.
THE CULTURE OF NARCISSISM points the way to a
world where new politics, new discipline and new love are
the only hope for a society moving helter-skelter towards
total self-absorption.

SOCIOLOGY/PSYCHOLOGY   0 349 12165 6   £1.75

THE
LEAN YEARS

BY RICHARD BARNET

THE LEAN YEARS is the first book to take an overall look at the world's resources – how much we have got, where they are, and who controls them. Richard Barnet, the distinguished economic and political analyst, unravels the scarcity puzzle, exploring the politics of the 'petroleum economy', revealing the role of the giant oil companies and evaluating the energy alternatives to OPEC oil. He examines the changing face of global power and the struggle for food, water and mineral resources which we can expect in the coming lean years, and reports on the role of the multinational corporations in the world employment crisis. In addition, he discusses the politics of a world in transition, the consequences of the growing industrialisation of labour worldwide, and the absurdities of scarcity in a world of plenty. And, finally, he offers positive proposals for reorganising global resource systems to meet the needs of Earth's burgeoning population.

CONSERVATION/ECONOMICS   0 349 10238 4   £2.50

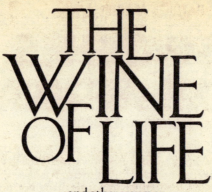

THE WINE OF LIFE

and other essays on
SOCIETIES, ENERGY
& LIVING THINGS

HAROLD J. MOROWITZ

'. . . a delight to read' CARL SAGAN

Dr Harold J. Morowitz, a distinguished professor of Molecular Biophysics at Yale University, offers a delightful blend of scientific fact and literary fancy in this collection of essays which has already been hailed as a contemporary classic. Filled with infectious curiosity and unpretentious wisdom, THE WINE OF LIFE is the most lively, lucid work of scientific commentary to appear since Lewis Thomas's LIVES OF A CELL.

'Dr Morowitz' pieces on scientific exposition are some of the wisest, wittiest, and best informed that I have read . . . I was deeply impressed' *C. P. Snow*

'A zest for life in general and the scientific life in particular, a wry slant on human foibles, and a sense of moral purpose flavour these short essays . . . these are the expressions of a thoughtful, intelligent man willing to take a stand on important issues'
Kirkus Reviews

SCIENCE   0 349 12386 1   £1.95

PATRICK MARNHAM

DISPATCHES FROM AFRICA

'We fear Africa because when we leave it alone, it works,'
says the author of this provocative book. Patrick
Marnham shows how outsiders – British, Russian,
American, French and Chinese – have repeatedly tried to
alter a land they do not understand. The relief workers,
scientists, businessmen, tourists and conservationists all
roam through Africa wreaking havoc as they go,
attempting to mould the continent into their numerous
images and ideals. Here are the elephants of Kenya and
their predators, the game wardens; the West African
outposts and their swollen populations of refugees; the
tourists of Africa, who come to enjoy the 'primitive life'
by observing a tribe which is desperately trying to flee
from them; the citizens of Bamako, building their houses
at night only to watch them being bulldozed the next
morning; and Gambia, a country of eight barristers and
no psychiatrists, where the British Ambassador's grant
ignored the inadequate hospitals and instead equipped a
new cricket team.

DISPATCHES FROM AFRICA reveals a country
beset by illogical boundaries, horribly mismanaged
financial aid and comically incompetent government
structures. But the true brilliance of the book is its ability
to allow still another Africa to seep through. The Africa of
powerful ideas and raw energy which, for reasons of
politics and ignorance, have gone awry. This Africa is a
land of Northern ineptitude superimposed on an inherent
native harmony.

'This shrewd, acrid book is an excellent antidote to the usual
guff written on Africa' *Sunday Telegraph*

WORLD AFFAIRS   0 349 12280 6   £1.95

JUST SOME OF THE TITLES ON THE ABACUS LIST:

THE WAPSHOT CHRONICLE	John Cheever	£1.95 ☐
WOMEN: PSYCHOLOGY'S PUZZLE	Joanna Bunker Rohrbaugh	£2.95 ☐
A GERMAN LOVE STORY	Rolf Hochhuth	£1.95 ☐
DISPATCHES FROM AFRICA	Patrick Marnham	£1.95 ☐
WEAPONS	Russell Warren Howe	£3.95 ☐
THE SIDMOUTH LETTERS	Jane Gardam	£1.75 ☐
SMALL IS BEAUTIFUL	E. F. Schumacher	£1.95 ☐
A GUIDE FOR THE PERPLEXED	E. F. Schumacher	£1.75 ☐
THE ARABS	Thomas Kiernan	£2.95 ☐
TO HAVE OR TO BE	Erich Fromm	£1.75 ☐
WORLDS IN COLLISION	Immanuel Velikovsky	£2.95 ☐

All Abacus books are available at your local bookshop or newsagent, or can be ordered direct from the publisher. Just tick the titles you want and fill in the form below.

Name _____

Address _____

_____

Write to Abacus Books, Cash Sales Department, P.O. Box 11, Falmouth, Cornwall TR10 9EN

Please enclose cheque or postal order to the value of the cover price plus:

UK: 40p for the first book plus 18p for the second book and 13p for each additional book ordered to a maximum charge of £1.49.

OVERSEAS: 60p for the first book plus 18p per copy for each additional book.

BFPO & EIRE: 40p for the first book, 18p for the second book plus 13p per copy for the next seven books, thereafter 7p per copy.

Abacus Books reserve the right to show new retail prices on covers which may differ from those previously advertised in the text or elsewhere, and to increase postal rates in accordance with the PO.